POKER - 101 WAYS TO WIN

By Andy Nelson

PokerBook Press

P.O. Box 17851, Boulder, Colorado

POKER - 101 WAYS TO WIN

Manufactured in the United States of America

First Printing - June, 1994

All material presented in this book is offered as information to the reader. While this material is believed to be accurate, neither the author nor the publisher make any claim to it being 100% reliable in all situations. The reader is advised to use his discretion in the application of the principles suggested. There is absolutely no inducement to gamble intended or implied.

ISBN 0-945983-22-0

10 9 8 7 6 5 4 3 2 1

TABLE OF CONTENTS

SECTION TWO

EMOTIONAL CONTROL 29

SECTION THREE

SECTION FOUR

SECTION FIVE

GENERAL POKER PHILOSOPHY TO HELP YOU WIN 133

Introduction

Life at the poker table just ain't easy. That is the long and the short of it. One has to tolerate obnoxious players, long runs of rotten cards, terrible playing conditions, bad food and tedious hours. So why are we hooked on this game? Some of us call it fun.

This book is my attempt to share the burden. We who play this absurd game need lots of help. Maybe this book will offer some bandages for our wounds, a tourniquet to stop the bleeding. Blood is particularly evident in low-limit poker. If this is your first book written by Andy Nelson, you should know that all of my writings are for the low-limit player.

Use this book as preparation for your Friday night game or your next session at the card palace. Read one chapter or several before you leave home and think about the suggestions as you drive to the game. The intention of this author is to help get your mind off the daily grind of problems and focused on the demands of poker. I don't suggest reading the book in one or two sittings. Take your time. Read and digest a few thoughts and then come back to the book later.

My goal is to provide you with a resource book, a book that will stimulate your thinking and bring to mind new and better ways of coping with other players and the way the cards run. I believe this book will increase your win *percentage* and the amount of money you win over the course of a year and a lifetime. These are tips that have been gleaned from my years of struggle.

I have divided the book into five sections. When you are having a problem in one of the areas covered, look first in that section. I want to be able to help you with tips that you can take to the table and provide positive solutions to tough questions.

I wish you well!

Planning

It takes a heap of living to make a house a home. It also takes a heap of work to enable a person to play consistently winning poker. I have placed the Planning section first because planning should be the first consideration. A reflective player who wants to move beyond the recreational player style must absolutely do some thinking, studying and pondering.

I suggest spending time visualizing the game and the players you usually play with. Go over what is the best way to play a certain starting hand. Focus on how to apply certain concepts, ideas like: When should you check-raise? When to slow play? When to drive out players? And when you want them to call?

Planning has a vital place in becoming a winner.

1

Be The Architect

Many, many forces form and structure our lives. We come into a world as babies without a choice of who our parents will be. We are molded by these people we call Mom and Dad. However, these are usually ordinary people with problems and troubles of their own. These people are major factors in our lives.

Despite this chance kind of beginning in life we can, and should, become the "captains of our own ships." For instance, we can design and shape our educations, our careers. We can, to some extent, structure the kind of relationships that we enter into. We can even be the architects to some degree of our future. This is what I call "being the architect of our lives."

One very important point I try to make with each poker class and each poker student I teach, is to tell my students that they have the choice to formulate their own poker future. We each carry within us the tools to make ourselves successful poker players. The game of poker is wonderful because it rewards skillful play. *We all have the capacity to become skillful players!* By learning to play skillfully, we can add a substantial source of income to our lives.

To be your own successful poker architect, you must first of all practice the art of patience. This is the hardest of all the lessons to master. We have such a desire to compete. We want to take a shot at winning each and every pot. This is what makes the game of poker so attractive and so profitable for the astute player. When we learn to overcome that urge to compete for pots that we have no business being in, we have a much better chance of ending the night with a win.

When you play in a game that is seven handed, *if the luck factor is exactly equal,* how often should you win a hand? The obvious answer is the best one, once out of seven times. If this is true, then why in the world are we wasting money trying to win the hands that we don't have a good percentage chance to win? Yet we all know that most players are playing extremely marginal hands, hoping to catch some miracle card and give them the win. A skillful player does not compete in hands that he does not have the best chance to win. He is patient! He waits until he catches the right starting cards before he puts more money in the pot. If he notices that a good player raises and he himself has a better-than-average hand, yet not a premium hand, he throws his hand away. He does not want to risk his money against the better hand. He is patient. He will wait for the correct moment when *he* will have the best hand. Then he will be extremely aggressive and take control of that hand. He *KNOWS* that if he plays carefully, waiting for his moment, he will eventually win. In the meantime, he is peaceful and quiet, knowing the flow of the cards will make him the winner.

Again and again I see research by computer that testifies to the assertion that the player who is willing to wait will become successful. What was noteworthy regarding this research was that the average players won two and three times as many pots as the good players, but the average player always lost money. It is not the number of pots you win! It is the amount of money you win that counts. So wait for the right moment, the moment when you get the best starting hand, before you invest your money. Be the architect of your own profitable poker enterprise. Be a winner!

2

Game Preparation

On your way to a poker game, do you drive on an interstate highway? Is the traffic vicious? Does driving demand all of your energy and attention? If these problems in driving are true for you, then you need to make some mental adjustments when you arrive at the poker place. To have to focus all your attention on the job of driving means that you can't use that time for preparation for the game.

Advanced game preparation has a direct impact on one's win percentage and total amount won for the year. Remember to take some time to review your game strategy. Here are just a few things to go over in your mind:

STARTING HANDS

Remind yourself of which cards you can play where. In fixed position games, this job is just a tad easier. Remind yourself to play only premium hands in early position. Be cautious with marginal hands except in late position in unraised pots. Review which hands you can call with when a raise is made.

In stud games where position can fluctuate each betting round, position is just as important for calls or raises with marginal hands. Big hands often play themselves, but big hands are few and far between. It is the marginal hands that cause problems but also offer good opportunities for profit. However, marginal hands cannot (repeat, cannot) be played indiscriminately. To call with a low pair and moderate kicker in early position in a Seven Card Stud game is not smart.

Whatever your game, think about which hands you can play from all the positions.

VISUALIZE

I certainly don't claim to understand the mystical parts of a card game, but I am a believer in the value of visualizing. I picture myself winning a pot, catching great starting hands that improve to win the pot. I then engage in a bit of fantasy where I am involved in a huge pot and the dealer is pushing it to me.

In my opinion, visualizing is a vital part of booking a win. Please don't ask me why it works. I just do it and it appears to make something positive happen. Try it.

PLAN A NEW MOVE

We should all be in the process of developing new plays. Taking a few moments for game prep is an ideal time to think up a new method of playing a certain hand. Think also about certain plays for situations that tend to repeat. Plan different tactics for these situations.

In almost all locations, you will be playing with a certain number of regular players. It is a good idea to review what you know about as many of these regular players as possible. If you can't get a fix on individual players, think about certain classes of players. Some recreational players play a lot alike. Analyze how these people play and what is the best way to counter.

RELAX

Perhaps the most profitable technique of all is to work on relaxation. Lower your shoulders, take a few deep breaths, *KNOW* that you are a good player. Convince yourself that a bad beat or two is not going to upset you. You know that the cards will come and your good hands will hold up. Expect it - you will find it will work just the way you want it to.

3

Be As Good As You Think You Are

The game of poker is truly fascinating. Yet within this game of poker, it seems to me that women have a distinct advantage because they can avoid a lot of the male macho thing. Women, I believe, can evaluate themselves without having to take an attitude of superiority.

Have you noticed that even a novice male player seems to exude an aura of mastery over the game? Despite his bravado, the novice player knows so very little about the nuances of the game. He makes mistakes that are often costly. Yet he truly believes he comprehends the game completely. This attitude is unbelievably expensive. A friend of mine describes this phenomenon as, "He doesn't know he doesn't know." That hits the nail exactly on the head.

Let's say a person decides to be a songwriter and composes a piece of music to sell to a publisher. He sends the creation off to be reviewed. If the writer does not have the talent to write music, the publisher sends the piece back with a rejection notice. That rejection notice is a clear message.

Let's say a person decides to write the great American novel and spends months and months in the composition of this manuscript. He sends the manuscript to an agent, who sends it back with an honest critique, basically saying this work is terrible. That message is clear.

9

Now let's say a person wants to create and sell a newsletter. He goes to the computer store and buys a good computer and the appropriate software. He has a friend install the software and sits down to make his fortune creating this newsletter. He discovers, however, that mastering the computer will take hundreds of hours, days of concentrated study, before he can even get started on the artistic masterpiece.

These above illustrations let the person know that he or she needs a *lot* of work to become accomplished. These illustrations tell us we are not as good as we think we are. Someone tells us in crystal clear terms we need to work hard to improve. This type of confrontational message is not true in poker. There is no bell that sounds, no message from God written on the wall that says, "Improve or you will lose your precious derriere." Nobody is telling the poker player, "Don't play leapfrog with a unicorn. It could do damage to some vital organ." The poker player needs to know which game to play and how to play it.

My advice is to do your homework and work to admit your weaknesses and mistakes. Take the advice of poker experts who will tell you poker is an incredibly complex game. Don't allow your ego to get in the way of profit. This game requires a long apprenticeship so don't fall into the trap of thinking you are better than you are. In fact, become as good as you think you are. Remember the old saying, "The easiest way to get rich is to buy people for what they are worth and sell them for what they think they are worth."

Stay in the games you can beat. Never go into a situation where you are outgunned. Don't be so desperate for action that your ego defines your play. Let your head, not your ego, rule your game.

4

Motivation Is The Key To Winning (Part One)

Colorado Cal had played poker for years and years. And for years and years, Colorado Cal lost money. He didn't lose each and every time. By no means. Sometimes he got on a heater and won for weeks on end. But there was never a year that Colorado Cal ended up with a win.

We should certainly ask *why* Cal lost consistently. Maybe we could learn something. Maybe we could find a way to improve our game.

Colorado Cal loved to play! Loving to play poker is not in and of itself a serious defect. However, Cal loved to play all the hands he was dealt. As a famous poker author has already written, "He never met a hand he didn't like." Playing a lot of hands is a serious flaw. The ability to lay down a hand is crucial for winning at poker. Colorado Cal would look at his hole cards and would find all kinds of excuses to play. The excuse he used a lot was, "Maybe I can draw out on him."

One day over a cup of coffee, I asked Cal how a certain player named Steve played. Cal answered, "I have no idea. I never watch the other players. I guess I am not motivated enough to study their play." That last remark is the clue we need to figure out why Cal loses. The word "motivation" is a fundamental factor in winning poker. Are you motivated? Are you motivated enough to study other players? Do you keep a journal to log your observations of regular players? Are you motivated enough to study the best way to play a hand? Do you pay attention to position? Do you get out of the hand when you are beat? These are just a few of the things better players do, so let's look at each one in a bit more depth.

STUDY THE HABITS OF OTHER PLAYERS

If you are truly motivated you will soon notice that some players will slow play the big pairs in Texas Hold 'Em. However, they will often raise with them *after* the flop. Can you name three players who do that?

Again in Hold 'Em, some players will call a raise with any two suited cards. In Seven Card Stud, some players will call with any pair, even with another one of their cards showing. That puts them in the position of severe underdog because they are drawing for only one card in the deck. In Omaha, some players will raise with a pair of aces and call all the way to the river with no improvement from the community cards. Some players will play a lot stronger when they are in late position than when they are first to act. Some players will raise with good draw hands. Some players will check-raise with draw hands.

Toby was such a player. When in a Hold 'Em game and when he flopped a flush draw in early position, he would invariably check-raise. His thinking was that if he got there, he wanted the pot to be a big one. Also, he felt that the check-raise would be a deceptive action. Needless to say, Toby had a page all his own in my journal. Regardless of which game you play, you need to know the weaknesses and the strengths of your fellow players.

5

Motivation Is The Key To Winning (Part Two)

These two chapters (Chapters 4 and 5) are about the level of motivation needed to prepare one to become a winning poker player. My friend, Colorado Cal, is an example of a player who was not terribly motivated.

The best poker players either have a great memory or they keep a journal. Since this book is for novice to intermediate players, let's not worry about the great memory part. That will come if you are motivated enough. It takes extra work to write some notes after each poker session, but that extra work is directly related to the level of your motivation. Are you willing to take the time, to expend the energy to become a better player? Just picture each player in your mind and write down some things they did, either good or bad. Did they re-raise with that pair of kings? Did they slow play the draw hands? Did they check-raise with two pair? When you start writing down these incidents you will program your mind to remember more and more of them. You will find yourself more alert to what is taking place. You are not just training yourself to remember a particular hand, you also will be developing your mind to notice what all the players did. Each and every hand has lessons to be learned.

Are you motivated enough to spend time thinking about different ways to play a full house? Most poker games have fast and furious action. You don't have time to explore each of several possible courses of action. If you have a plan in place, you can implement that plan instantly or you can choose one of several alternatives very quickly.

Suppose you catch rolled up trips in Seven Card Stud. Are you prepared to slow play them? Or what is the best way to play three of a kind when the pot is raised and re-raised before it gets to you? Should you also raise? Or will you likely make more money if you wait until fifth street to let them know you have a good hand?

If you have a pair of tens in an Omaha game and the flop comes with a red jack and the two black tens, how do you react? You have the best possible hand with little chance of getting beat by a royal flush or four jacks. The usual play is to only call until the next betting round. However, once in a while, when you flop a monster, lead bet it. That will probably mislead most of the players and make them cautious when you lead bet the next time.

Good position is power. You can make more money and lose less money if you play position correctly. It is easier in fixed position games like Texas Hold 'Em and Omaha Hold 'Em to keep position in mind. In random position games like Seven Card Stud, it takes a tad more motivation to keep remembering where you are in relation to the first person to act. The more people who act in front, the more knowledge you have of who has what.

The discipline to throw away marginal hands that are beat is tough to develop. It takes motivation to remind yourself that the old principle of good poker is true: *When you are beat, get out!* If you have the motivation to recall that axiom twenty or so times per poker session, you will cash out a lot more chips.

Remember Colorado Cal. He lacked motivation to learn how to play correctly and profitably. He lost money every year. You can learn from his experience and decrease your losses and increase your wins by becoming motivated to win. Choose good habits.

6

You Have To Show Up Every Day

The statement, "You have to show up every day" applies to successful and profitable poker. It doesn't mean you have to play poker every day. Let's be perfectly clear on that. To "show up every day" means to me that you bring into your life a certain level of dedication, a commitment to quality play, a resolution to win, a faithfulness to study and think about the game in a cosmic sense, and a trust that the mystical flow of cards will be a benefit to you.

"To show up every day" is a value statement that we make to ourselves. It tells us that we are willing to make a trade-off, the trade-off being time away from the couch watching a stupid sitcom in deference to applying some energy to thought and study, to be willing to spend some money for books, videos and computer software to improve our play. The trade-off of giving up certain habits we have, like haranguing novice players about a stupid play, about working on emotional control so we don't go on tilt. "To show up every day" means to put effort into the study of our opponents. It means taking time to keep accurate records of wins and losses, of keeping a journal of our opponents. "To show up every day" encompasses a value system that will dramatically change the way we play the game of poker. Instead of being a donator, one of the 95 percent of the players who do not win over the course of a year, we become winners. We become winners and we win the respect of our peers.

Let me illustrate what I mean by showing up every day. Julie was a softball player. Julie came from a borderline poverty situation with five brothers and sisters. The family was close and there was a lot of internal support. The kids knew there was only so much money to go around and they cooperated with each other in dividing the money that was available for sports.

Julie worked hard at her sport. She knew it was her ticket to a better life. After she became an All-American in softball, she began to work with disadvantaged kids. These kids were normal kids, always complaining about how bad they had it. They harped on their problems and disadvantages. With great eloquence, Julie would say, "Bull crap!"

She would tell them about her life on the wrong side of the tracks and would accept nothing from them except a full effort. She would say to them, "You have to show up every day or you will not amount to anything. Nothing comes easy. Just do it."

Doesn't that same philosophy apply to poker? It think it does. Try it, you'll like it.

7

The Mettle Of The Person

To me, there is nothing, I repeat, *Nothing* like a losing streak to test one's mettle. I am having a bad run of cards right now, and have had so for the past months. It gets very trying to sit down and play hour after hour, consistently depositing money into the game. It is a true test of my mettle to write down that loss time after time. Sometimes I can cope quite well with losing. Other times, I know that I have to get up and leave or I will become very irritated.

Lately, I haven't been able to get off ground zero. The cards are just not coming. Every hour I play it seems I have to dig deeper into my wallet. You all know this feeling of sinking slowly into the mire. This is the kind of lousy losing streak I am talking about. I am not speaking of the occasional evening of taking a loss. This streak has been going on for months.

One thing that helps me is to look at this losing streak as a challenge. Anyone can play good cards and win. A good player can exist on mediocre cards and still post a slim win or a very modest loss. The challenge for all of us is to weather a long, long stretch of bad cards and bad flops. This is a test of the mettle of my survival skills.

By "weathering" I don't mean sitting at the table brooding, scowling, grumbling and complaining. We have all heard players whining about the way the cards are coming. Hand after hand, hour after hour, they gripe. It is a chore to be near them. By weathering, I mean maintaining a cheerful attitude - passing the time by observing the play and making conclusions as to how each person is playing. Since this kind of a streak prohibits us from playing everything except the very best cards, we have lots of opportunity to observe. The challenge is to overcome ourselves and to surmount that awful feeling that comes with losing.

Another tactic I try to use is to play *extremely* conservatively when I first begin to play. When I sit down, I am careful to not take any chances with playing a marginal hand in poor or moderate position. I will play a marginal hand, say 10-jack offsuit (in Texas Hold 'Em) when I am on the button or in very late position, provided there have been no raises. Even very early in the session, I consider that 10-jack a reasonable investment. In those first few rounds, I want to play carefully and test the flow of the cards and the feel that I have for the table. I want to get a sense of how the other players are playing; is the game fired up, who is having a good day, and who is starting to tilt. If I should get big cards, especially suited cards, I will play them as I normally play. If I get beat with them, I become even more cautious. It is only when I win a pot or two that I start to change my play and risk. You have gathered that when I risk, I want to risk some money I have won and not my own initial bankroll.

Don't get me wrong. Sometimes I can't maintain this composure. Sometimes I look with envy and desire at the guy stacking the chips, and in my heart I despise him. But I have found that my best weapon to counter these emotions of craving is to remember that I win a lot and then to recall those feelings. I know the cards will turn and once again Lady Luck will pass my way. Until then, please send up a prayer to the poker god for me. I have had all I want of this bad streak.

8

Getting A Read On An Opponent

In any variety of low-limit poker, hand selection is the most important ingredient for a profitable session. As everyone knows, low-limit poker has lots of action. Lots and lots of players will play each and every hand they are dealt. Hence the advanced and expert players can seldom use their money as a weapon and drive players off the pot. Low-limit poker is usually show-down poker. Players will simply call you down with statements like "I will keep you honest."

A FIRST READ

Since starting hand selection is so important for profit, one of the first reads you can get on a player is what hands he selects to play from what position. In other words, what his or her requirements are for playing a hand. A careful watch on what hands a player chooses to play from early, middle and late position will tell you a lot about the overall poker skill of the player. I have found that some good players keep a log on regular opponents and make a particular note of what hands these players select to play. They write down the hands that are exposed by a certain player, along with comments on the action that led up to the play. Items of importance are position, where the raise was (if there was one), how big the pot was, and which player made the raise.

For instance, in Seven Card Stud, does an opponent call the opening bet with two big unsuited cards? Does he call with an ace in the hole? With two to a suit? If he calls with what appears to be a pair of sevens, does he call a raise from what appears to be a pair of kings or aces? Does he call with a pair of tens with another ten showing?

In Seven Card Stud, High/Low Split, does a player start with a two-card low? A small pair? Call a raise with an eight showing as his up card?

In Texas Hold 'Em, does he call with any two suited cards? Unsuited connectors? Will he raise (and re-raise) with the big premium pairs or does he usually slow play them?

In most cases, you can get a pretty good read on a player's level of skill by watching and noting what cards he turns over. When you get the opportunity to see a player's starting hand, you can mentally replay the hand, checking how the hand developed. This will give you a bit of a profile on what kind of play you can expect from him. If a player shows you only big cards and usually wins the pot when he plays, you must respect his play. If he or she makes a series of questionable calls and throws his hand away without showing, you must regard him as a calling station and seldom try to bluff him.

These are just a few ideas on reading opponents. Making a good estimate of the cards a player holds is essential for long-term profit. What time and energy you spend on learning to read players will pay off big time. More tips on reading players will come later.

9

Stop And Think Before You Call A Raise

Freddie has the blind in a low-limit game of Texas Hold 'Em. Freddie has a J-10 offsuit. He calls a raise made by Willie from the ninth position. It seems to me that Freddie's call was an appropriate investment because it appeared six others would also be in the pot. The flop comes J♦ 7♥ 6♠. Freddie bets out and four players call. The next card off is a 4♣. Again Freddie bets. He gets one caller before Willie raises. When the action gets back to him, Freddie grunts, peeks at his cards, rechecks the flop and dumps in his money to call the raise. That was *not* a good call.

The last card to flop is a K♥. Freddie checks and calls Willie's last bet. Willie turns over a pair of queens.

The most powerful way of communicating at the poker table is by raising. Therefore, when we get raised, we need to ask ourselves a couple of questions. Questions like: "Am I beat?" "If I put more money in the pot, will I be getting a fair return on my money?"

The vast majority of poker players automatically call a raise. This *automatic* call is wrong.

Let's go back to Freddie and his pair of Jacks. We know that even with top pair (before the last card), Freddie does not have a great hand. Willie is a good solid player. He is known to bluff only on rare occasions. His raise indicates a good hand. Some players in late position will raise with the middle pairs. I have never seen Willie do this. Willie, with his raise, is telling us that he has, *at the very least,* a pair of Jacks with a good kicker! Even if Willie had "only" A-J, K-J, or Q-J, Freddie was beat. More than likely, his raise before the flop and especially on 4th street, indicates an overpair.

The "automatic call" after the raise on fourth was what most of us do. We "automatically" dump in our money. In my opinion, the bets Freddie made after the flop and after the fourth card were appropriate. He had top pair. If no one else had a jack or an overpair, he had the best hand. However, he should have revaluated after the raise. There are several reasons to make a bet, one of them being to obtain information. Freddie was doing great, he made the correct bets, but he did not listen to the information he received.

Willie's raise was a powerful message. He was telling Freddie that he had him beat. Like most of us, Freddie did not listen to the message he was given. He could and should have saved two bets. Automatically throwing money in the pot is a terrible policy.

What Freddie should have done was review the hand. His thought process could have gone something like this: "Willie is a good player. He raised before the flop. He would not raise without a good hand. Certainly he knows I have a pair of jacks. What his raise means is that he has a pair of jacks beat. My only reasonably safe out is to pair my ten. It will cost me one bet to take that chance. Is there enough money in the pot to justify a call and hope to catch a ten? I have three tens to catch out of 46 unknown cards. That is about 15 to 1. I think it's time to quit."

My Uncle Sigurd used to say that saving money was the same as making money. Don't throw good money away. When the message comes across to us that we are beat, it's time to get out. We have paid for the message: don't ignore it. When a raise is made, pause a moment to think. The best course of action could very well be to fold.

10

Coping With A Check-Raise

Is check-raising against the rules of poker? Is it against the ethics of poker? Many, many people consider check-raising to be unethical or unsportsmanlike. A lot of home games do not permit it because of this evaluation of the check-raise. After all, would or should you check-raise a friend? That is certainly a viable question.

Most poker games played in casinos permit check-raising. When a poker player who has only played in home games that prohibit check-raising sits down in a casino game, he is at a disadvantage. He or she just hasn't had to cope with check-raising and is taken by surprise.

A couple of times, when I have check-raised someone, they looked at me with anger and frustration. One asked me, "You check-raise in a small game like this?" It was obvious he had not encountered it before. Since I was used to casino play, I was surprised by his reaction.

AWARENESS IS THE BEST DEFENSE

The best coping mechanism is to be aware that check-raising is part of that particular game. Make yourself aware that check-raising is permitted under house rules. If it is permitted, do not let it upset you when it happens. The players are playing within the rules and it is up to you to cope with it.

The next level of managing check-raising is to avoid obvious situations where you can be the victim. Many players use check-raising to shut down an overly aggressive player. I want you to be aggressive, but set some limits. If you have the habit of always betting when you are last to act, regardless of what kind of hand you have, you are quite susceptible to the check-raise. The better players will notice and let you build a pot for them by letting you bet and then check-raise. That is a legitimate tactic and I have used it many times. It has also been used against me. When you are getting check-raised consistently, check out your aggressiveness. It might be the problem.

SOME PLAYERS ENJOY THE CHECK-RAISE

My last suggestion is to make a note of which players use the check-raise. Some players use it more than others. Some players take great joy in check-raising. They think it is great fun and enjoy your overreaction. It is quite simple to make a mental note of who those players are and try to avoid situations where you are vulnerable. An ideal situation is for you to catch a big hand, get check-raised and then re-raise to win a bigger pot and teach the smart aleck a lesson.

When you are check-raised, be very careful that you do not become angry. If you let your temper flare, you are playing into the hands of smart players. They will take your chips. Beware.

11

Choosing Your Poker Table

On a few rare occasions I have played in a club where I had a choice of more than one table of a certain game at a certain limit. Unfortunately, the rest of the world is not like Nevada or California poker rooms. If you can play poker in a club that offers you even a choice of two tables at the limit you are comfortable with, consider yourself fortunate. Most of the rest of us either play in a home game or a one or two table club. The privilege of choosing your table offers you additional profit. "Ladies and gentlemen, choose your tables."

Consider this: A student of mine was progressing nicely after several weeks of private classes with me. In a $3 - $6 Texas Hold 'Em game, he was ahead $835 for a week. The next week he won $135 the first time he played. Then the ceiling crashed around his ears. He was ahead a bit over $100 when three new players came into the game. Each of the three loved to gamble and rock and roll. The cumulative impact on the game was substantial: 75 percent of the pots were capped before the flop and after the flop. The pots were huge as these players influenced the others to gamble with them. One average player caught some hands and cashed out $600 after two hours. My student, Les, did not have the experience to cope with this change in the complexion of the table. (He was still working on his betting strategy for his own hand and seldom could effectively read

25

another player.) He saw that these gamble guys were winning with trash hands, so he loosened up his starting requirements and tried to play with them. First mistake, right? Of course. As you have guessed, they cleaned Les for $350. He called me *early* the next morning to schedule a session.

"What should I have done?" Les moaned. "How can I cope with this kind of play?"

My answer was a question. "Did they have another table?"

"No."

"Then you should have quit rather than play their game. As of now, you do not have the experience to counter their aggressive tactics. Being a novice and consequently a solid rock type, they can read you like an open book. They can quote chapter and verse on your play after just a few moments. The best thing for you to do in this situation is quit the table."

It is like Christmas in July for experienced players to find a loose table with guys who love to gamble, but for Les it was disaster. Fortunately, Les is a sharp person and he will not make that mistake again.

Being able to choose from more than one table will make you money. Lots of times you will even be able to make more money at a slightly lower limit table that has fewer good players than a higher stakes game with pretty solid players. Look the people over. See how many players are involved at the beginning of the hand. If there are 70 to 80 percent playing, you have a good table. Also count the good players, the average players and the novices. Spend a few moments considering which ones will be easier. We often tend to sit with our buddies and not pay much attention to the other table. Keep an eye on the other tables. As the complexion changes, consider shifting. Easier players equates to easier money.

12

Beware The Bluffer

Beware the guy who plays an outrageous hand, who maybe raises with real rubbish and when he wins, makes a point of showing it to everyone at the table. Keep an eye on this guy. If his game is basically sound, if he usually only plays very strong hands, you can be pretty sure that when he reveals his hand, he is setting you up. It is a ploy. He wants to advertise to everyone that he just ran a successful bluff. He wants you to believe that he is a foolish player who is playing lots of junk. He is inviting you to call him down whenever he bets.

He is setting up a trap. He is baiting you. This is a clever player who is trying to play a head game with you. Beware of this person. He or she will soon have some of your chips unless you give him the credit he deserves. He has given you the tip that you need; he has told you that he has a deeper understanding of the game. This person has studied the human response to this kind of play and he is like the spider who says to the fly, "Come into my parlor so that we can talk."

THE PSYCHOLOGICAL GAME

Make no mistake, when we throw away a pretty decent hand after a guy bluffs us, it creates an impression. We had the best hand and the person just outplayed us. Beware of the emotional reaction of saying to yourself, "I'll never let him do that again." If you say that to yourself, you are playing his game. He has set and baited his trap and you are about to be ensnared.

This person has a good knowledge of how humans react to certain circumstances. He has created that set of circumstances and is now waiting for victims to react the way he wants them to. Like the spider, he has built an elaborate web and is waiting for the fly. Beware.

Most of the time, he will have a good hand.

If you have read the situation right, that he is a solid player who has displayed his trash hands deliberately, from now on he will only show down very good hands. Like the spider, you are his lunch, his fly who accepts the invitation to enter the web.

If this player is a wild and foolhardy one, the circumstances are entirely different. By showing everyone his junk hand, this person is telling you that he considers himself a clever player. He has an ego situation that can be profitable for you. He will regularly play trash and will usually be a generous donator to your game. Do a careful evaluation and beware the bluffer who knows how to manipulate you, and rejoice over the bluffer who just likes to speed around and show you how good he is.

A TIP

Notice how the good bluffer has set your teeth on edge. You can learn how to use this tactic by carefully evaluating yourself, your emotions and reactions to certain stimuli. When you recognize your responses are anger or joy, you can usually translate those responses into what almost everyone would feel under that set of circumstances. Watch you own emotions. This is the tip-off on how to use those emotions to manipulate your opponents.

Emotional Control

Sometimes it is not a pretty sight. The guy in number seven seat flopped the nut flush in a low-limit Omaha High/Low split game. He also had the nut wheel draw. He made the wheel on the turn and lost the high end of the hand when the board paired the three on the river. He ended up with one-third of half of the pot. His face got red. He tried his best to stay calm. He got up and walked around the table three times, all the while lambasting the dealer. When he finally sat down, he did not even look at his cards before he raised. This guy was far out, totally out of control.

His substantial stack of chips lasted twenty minutes. Then he slammed his chair into the aisle and he stormed off into the night.

What is the lesson here?

Don't let this happen to you. Low-limit poker is alive with this kind of situation. Unless you accept the risks and let them flow off your back, you are in danger. Beware!

13

Tilt Prevention

Harry was steamed and everyone knew it. Harry had flopped a black ace on the board to go with his pair of red aces in the pocket. This was a low-limit ($3-$6) Hold 'Em game and the complete flop was A♣-6♥-10♦. Harry had the opportunity to raise after the flop and merely called because he wanted to keep the players in. He slow played that set of aces into a full-blown tilt. A pretty little lady named Billie was on the button and she called before the flop raise and the $3 bet after the flop with 3♥-4♥. Bless her soul.

You have already guessed that the turn card gave that pretty lady a straight draw. She caught the seven of clubs on 4th street and got a red five on the river. Billie giggled as she stacked the chips and tossed the dealer two dollars.

Meanwhile, Harry percolated. In my head, I considered how I could take advantage of poor Harry's temper tantrum. It ain't nice to do that, but when I am at the poker table, I don't have a bleeding heart. I check the nice guy part of me at the door. When I see an opening, I go for it and encourage you to do the same. If you can't cope with a tilt, stay out of a poker game. Especially low-limit poker. Low-limit poker is a draw-out game and you will lose a lot of pots on the last card. Tilt and low-limit go together like jelly and peanut butter.

TILT COSTS MONEY

While Harry was hot with anger, several of us individually plotted to get some of the chips he was bound to give away. Sure enough, he played several trash hands and dumped $150 before he stalked off into the night. Those trip aces cost him money and his good humor.

Remember the first rule of tilt prention: When you feel yourself starting to tilt, re-group. Few of us can afford the luxury of a full-sized, overgrown tilt. That anger, that disgust over bad play will surely cost you money. Sure, Billie was an idiot to stay to draw for those two perfect cards, but that makes low-limit poker what it is, wonderfully profitable. The Billies of the world will pay for your next Brooks Brothers suit. But not if you tilt out and throw away those well-earned chips.

WHAT DOES RE-GROUP MEAN? IT MEANS:

A. Get up and walk. Have a talk with yourself. Remind yourself that the best thing that could happen to you in this game was when Billie won that pot. Now she will stay in with each and every two card draw and all kinds of crazy stuff. Those chips Billie has in her stacks are live. They will be back in action soon!

B. Go wash your face. Talk to a friend. Have a cup of coffee. Sit out at least a full round and get yourself mentally ready to play again.

C. When you do sit down again, *play tight!* For a few rounds, take no chances. Play the most conservative poker you are capable of playing. That will help your own mental stability and also confuse your opponents who are expecting you to be irrational.

14

Survival Skills

One of the great statesmen and most quoted men of the twentieth century was Winston Churchill. He was the Prime Minister when England faced the greatest challenge in its history. He understood the need to instill backbone into the people of Britain so that England would survive in World War II. Let me quote:

Victory at all cost, victory in spite of all terror, victory however long and hard the road may be; for without victory there is no survival.

Unfortunately, a poker player is often faced with plain ordinary, garden-variety, vanilla-flavored survival. Whatever level of skill you possess, regardless of mental acumen, notwithstanding the amount of study and dedication, it appears there is at least one period or more in every career when one's very survival is threatened. I believe this also applies to every person in whatever career choice they make. Since this is a book about poker and how to win at poker, I will concentrate on how one must first of all recognize the crisis of survival and, more important, how to survive a tragic turn of cards/luck.

RECOGNIZE THE FACT OF CRISIS

In another chapter (Chapter 18) in this book, I write about the shift of fortunes and recognizing if the cards have turned against you or you have turned against the cards. In my experience, I find it is usually a combination of both. A flow of bad cards often precipitates a flow of bad play. I will not say it is easy to determine what comes first, bad cards or bad play. It is a most difficult task to be completely objective in analyzing the interfacing of luck and skill. Usually the recognition of the crisis comes from poverty, reinforced by a serious review of your won-lost record.

COPING WITH SURVIVAL

I believe you would agree that a most critical matter is coping with a tragic turn of the cards. We *must* know how to survive?

The first suggestion I have is to lower your expectations. It is a true statement that expectations are a key to happiness. Don't expect to win much. Be willing to quit with a very modest win. In fact, be *happy* with a modest win. Adjust your thinking so that you are in a famine and a bowl of soup might be all that you can expect.

The second suggestion is to critically review your discipline. Do not let your emotions rule. Do not moan and groan. Pick only the best starting hands and abandon your hand if the situation turns dangerous.

My third suggestion is to be extremely careful to find the optimal conditions. Don't play in any game where you are not a favorite. Don't play in any game that is beyond your current bankroll. If you have to sit and wait for the better game, do so. Remember, this is survival. You cannot afford the luxury of deluding yourself that you can now beat every game. When money is in short supply, don't risk. Face the fact that every player in the world has a crisis and this is yours. How you cope with the crisis will determine much of your future success.

15

Rules To Live By At The Poker Table

Stone walls do not a prison make nor iron bars a cage.
(Richard Lovelace)

Most of us chafe against the rules because we feel rules limit our freedom. This is true, rules do place limitation on us. A sort of prison. When the traffic light is red, the rule is for us to stop and wait for the green light. That red light restricts my freedom to drive anywhere I want at any speed I chose. However, that red light also protects me from being hit by other drivers when I have the green light. If I should run the red light and get caught by the police, I must pay the fine that society has decided is the penalty for such an infraction. That is the penalty that enforces the rule and helps keep me and others in line so our society can function in an orderly manner.

When I break the rules, I pay. That is the "prison" that our community has agreed on, and it has proved workable. That is prison without walls and without iron bars.

FORMULATE YOUR OWN POKER RULES

It is in your best interest to have some solid rules to live by when you sit down at the poker table. These rules will help keep you from paying the price of losing money. Remember, when you break the rules, you pay.

Here are some of my rules which might give you some ideas for your own:

A. I must have the resources to play correctly.

> 1. The money I lay out for chips is not the rent money, the food money or money promised to someone else. If the money I use to buy chips is "committed" money, I will feel some restraints in my betting practices. Playing with short money or committed money is a self-defeating practice.

> 2. I must be in a good mental state to play. That solid emotional state is a valuable resource to have when the game begins. If I am upset by some stuff that is happening at home or I am mad at the bank or the floor man or another player, I don't play. It costs money to play when I am upset and losing will only cause me further unhappiness!

> 3. One of the resources that I use is a talk with myself before I enter the action. (I sometimes wonder if other people talk to themselves.) I remind myself to go easy at the beginning. Get a fix on some of the players before I enter a pot. Do not play marginal hands until I have a good feel for the game. (And maybe not at all.)

B. I have a limit to how much money I am willing to lose in whatever limit I am playing.

C. I mentally review what I know about each player that I have played with.

Breaking the "rules" can be costly. Just try speeding away from a patrolman, if you don't believe me. So don't be stupid. Play smart and live with the rules. Those stone walls also give you a sense of security.

16

Remedial Poker

Oh, how it hurts to take beat after beat, session after session. The pain is real, the frustration valid. "How do we get into such quandaries," we ask? How indeed? How can we run along day after day, doing okay, logging a 70 to 80 percent win ratio and suddenly the well runs dry.? We can't catch a starting hand, or worse, do catch good starting cards and get tromped by the little old lady from Busted Lance, Oklahoma. Hand after hand, hour after hour, our monetary blood sucked by the vampires. This is a job for — trumpets and drum roll please — *Remedial Man*.

As the futility mounts, take a time-out. Call the "T". When the going gets tough, get a good grip on yourself. You are in a battle against monsters and demons. When you cut off one of the heads of the fire-breathing dragon, another seven heads grow in its place. It is time to go back to school, time to take a good long look at the big picture.

An old friend of mine, a tall, gangly Swede, had a favorite saying. It was, "When the going gets too tough for everyone else, it is just right for me." It is that kind of an attitude that we all need to have to survive in this poker environment. You can make book on it, there will be times that poker will drive you a bit nuts. Not only will you talk to yourself, you will slobber, stutter and speak in foreign tongues. Be prepared!

THE FIRST RULE

My first rule in regard to surviving the poker environment is: *I am my own worst enemy*. Sure, the cards run colder than an Alaskan doorknob. Sure, the idiots are drawing to incredible long shots and making them. Sure, I should have zigged when I zagged. I move into a hot seat and it turns cold. I have the dealer change decks. I walk around my chair. I do everything to change the way the cards are coming and nothing works, but I must first look to myself to see how I am contributing to the problem. That is why I need time to think and re-evaluate.

THE SOLUTION

What seems to work best for me is to go back to the books, to review Sklansky, Brunson, Caro. I look at the videos, listen to the tapes. I take time away from the table to get back to the basics, In short, I do *Remedial Poker*.

A second thing that helps me is to ask a friend to evaluate my play. I have him sit behind me and I show him my cards, and he watches how I bet and react to what is happening. This seems to work.

As I am writing this, I am in the midst of the dark ages. Yesterday, the only set of trips I flopped all day was run down by a pretty lass who backdoored a diamond flush. That was what sent me out the door. I went to another casino and sat down in a Seven Card Stud, High/Low game and caught two hands and split two other pots. You see, I cut my poker eye teeth on Seven Card split and feel I can win at that game eight out of ten times. Sure enough, I was right. I played tight and aggressive when I had the edge and refused to be drawn into chancy situations. That modest win boosted my spirits immensely. I feel now that if I can't catch in Texas Hold 'Em, I can move easily to Seven Stud Split and wait out the futility.

17

Be Cool

Almost all the people that I meet at the poker table are people I can like. Since most of the poker I play is low-limit poker, most of the people are pretty much like me. There are blue collar people, white collar people, retired folks, people of color, rich guys, slick dressers, handsome dudes and pretty women. Sure, some of the arrogant rascals give me a problem, but I think to myself that these poor slobs must have a weak ego to protect, so they come off as pompous. Hey, that's okay most of the time because I understand they have a need. We all have needs that must be met. Mine happen to be different than theirs. I figure if I am tolerant, perhaps they will be tolerant of me.

As I said, I like *most* of the folks. The ones who can get to me sometimes are those that lay on a bad beat. These are the ones who play the long shots and occasionally get there and beat me out of the pot that I figured was mine. Everyone has heard the stories about the bad beat artist, the suck out devils that inhabit the low-limit poker scene.

The purpose of this chapter is not to whine about bad beats, but to help develop strategies to "be cool." I am trying to pass on a strategy that has helped me manage my emotions when one of them sticks the stiletto into my hand as I reach for the pot he just smuggled away from me.

TOLERATION

I have entitled my strategy "toleration." That describes what I have developed, and continue to develop, as a mechanism to defeat this type of play and what keeps me from going on tilt because of their tactics. First of all, the suck-out crowd is part and parcel of low-limit play. Accept that. Live with that. Don't moan and complain. The reality is that bad beats have been and always will be a factor in low-limit play. Now, let's develop strategies that work to defeat them.

My strategy is simply this: *I don't let it bother me!* "Oh yeah?" you say. "That is a crock." Believe me, I have worked a lot on this because bottom feeders are a part of the challenge of low-limit poker and, in order to win, I have to defeat them. So I have worked on controling my emotional response. As you know, the emotional response to a bad beat is mayhem. I have actually learned to be cool, to say, "Good hand." Now we both know that I don't mean, "Good hand." I am thinking, "Good hand, Stupid." But I *really* don't let it affect me. I just hope that person doesn't go home early because I want my money back.

MY LEVEL OF TOLERANCE (TODAY)

I am almost always able to tolerate up to three bad beats in one session. When I get the third one, I am thinking *very seriousy* about changing tables or quitting for the day. If my emotional control is in good shape, I will stay for a while longer. What I am trying to do is to be able to say to myself, "Now I can tolerate four bad beats." Then I want to work up to five bad beats without losing my cool. You follow? I don't want to change them, I want to change me. I want to get better and better at toleration. I want to be so cool, no set of cruel circumstances will blow me away.

18

Is It Me Or Is It The Cards?

Oh, how I love to blame the cards when I lose! Those #&*+#@&!%*# things just don't have the sense to come in out of the rain. Time after time those cards let me down. In Hold 'Em, when I have the nut flush draw in hearts, black cards come on the flop. Or I get two hearts on the flop and never see another heart. That nut draw costs me some money and I will gladly pay it, but when those nut draws fail to come in time after time it sure gets discouraging. It makes me curse the cards.

LOOK FIRST TO YOURSELF

However, I need to be really sure that it is the cards that are causing me to lose consistently. The most honest and important question to ask is, "Is it me or is it the cards? When I ask that question of myself and am quite clear on the answer, the answer I get is usually me. Humble medicine, I know.

Sure, I know that those cards run badly for some period of time. No one wins all the time. That tells me that cards fluctuate — they run hot and they run cold. However, a good player takes that fluctuation into account and accommodates himself to the bad runs as well as the good ones.

41

I have gone through periods of play when I was convinced that the cards hated me. Perhaps I had offended the poker goddess, the lady that is known as Luck. However, when I honestly asked the question, "Is it me or is it the cards?" the answer came up *me* most of the time. That answer generally was validated when I re-evaluated my play and modified my approach. Then, lo and wonder, I started to win again. And, boy, was that better than a sharp stick in the eye.

LOOK ALSO AT THE CARDS

It isn't *always* bad play on my part. Everyone goes through periods of bad cards, regardless of what game they play. When you can't pick up a decent starting hand, you just have to be able to discipline yourself to wait and wait. To compromise our starting requirements is a disaster waiting to occur. The only true option is to delay spending our chips until we have a good shot at winning the pot. Each and every chip has value when we go to the cashier's cage. When we insist on playing poor-to-marginal hands when we are frustrated, we won't carry away the chips that should be ours. My goal is to always carry away just as many chips as I possibly can, day after day after day. When the cards run good for me, I will have a great time. When the cards run average, I hope to concentrate on each and every hand and walk away with a modest win. When the cards run terrible, I want to hold my emotions in a vice-like grip, cut my losses and maybe even mark down a small amount in the plus column. I want to get to the point where I can *always* answer "cards" to the question, "Is it me or is it the cards?"

19

Low-Limit Frustration

When is a bad beat a bad beat? I suggest that in low-limit games a bad beat almost doesn't exist. Before you pick up that ax to throw it at me, hear me out.

The huge attraction for low-limit poker is action. Or should I say *Action*? Anyone who sits down to play and has a terrible run of cards can lose a good-sized bankroll, but the usual situation is even a terrible player will lose only a modest amount. What this means is that the potential loss for any given session is well within the financial reach of most players. That translates into lots and lots of action.

One feature of low-limit are the long-shot draws. There are just an incredible number of long-shot draws. That usually means more than one long-shot draw on each and every hand. It is a truth that even a long-shot draw like a 1 in 47 comes in once in 47 times. However, when two or three players are drawing at that long-shot, it is several times more likely to come in any particular hand. Like it or not, long-shot draws are part of the landscape in low-limit poker.

The ideal situation for the good player is to have the best hand at each betting round. The problem with low-limit poker is that sometimes those draw-out players (or suck-out players) will hit their long-shot draw. Then you have the best hand at every betting round, except at the very end. Lots of players call this draw out a bad beat. I do not. To me, these so-called bad beats are just part of what happens in every low-limit game. It is nothing special to get a good hand beat by some ding-dong with more money than brains. When this happens to you, my advice is to throw your hand away and say, "Nice hand." Don't let the crazies get under your skin or you are in deep do-do. Say to yourself, "Andy said there is no such thing as bad beats, only unfortunate circumstances." Talk to yourself until you convince yourself you are the much better player and that the flow of the cards will take care of you and make you the winner.

20

How To Counter A Stupid Play

I was playing in a low-limit Texas Hold 'Em game and a lady called a raised pot with 2-3. The flop came K-A-6. I had flopped top two pairs with my A-K and I had the dealer's button. It was bet in early position, this lady named Gloria called, and I raised. She called again. The next card was 3. It was checked to me and I bet. Gloria called. The last card was 3. It was checked around to me, so I bet. Gloria check-raised me with her three threes. As she scooped in the pot, my mouth was gaping. This had to be one of the most stupid plays in the history of the world and yet she stacked my money!

My purpose is not to relate to you a bad beat story. I hate bad beat stories as much as anyone. My intention is for you to be prepared for this kind of foolishness that goes on in low-limit poker.

My friend George has been known to go ballistic when he loses his chips to a person who has made a stupid play. A guy, Lee, in the big blind, called his raise in a Texas Hold 'Em game with 3-7. The flop came A♣–J♣–5♣. George had flopped the top two pairs from late position and bet. The big blind, Lee, called. The next card was a nothing; again Lee called. The last card was a club and Lee won with his three of clubs. George hit the after burner and orbited the earth a few times and proceeded to lose the rest of his chips in the next half hour.

PREPARATION

What can you say to George? I mean, that was one hell of a beat! Lee at no time, *at no time,* had a decent reason to call. Yet he won the pot. Sometimes low-limit poker can be hard on your vocabulary, on your blood pressure and your stomach lining.

Low-limit poker is like surviving in an arctic region, where preparation is a necessity. If you are not prepared to control your emotions after this kind of beat, you lose. Big time. Readiness to withstand the loss of your money is not an easy task. The problem to focus on is the protection of the remainder of your financial stash.

The preparation for a stupid play is quite comparable to preparation for starting hand selection. Instead of remembering which hands you can play from which positions, you need to be prepared for a fluctuation in emotions. One must be careful not to become angry and reprimand the poor stupid wretch for his incredible play. What you should practice is to visualize yourself being perfectly calm and say something like, "That was a nice hand, sir." You need to play that over and over in your head until you can say it without a trace of bitterness.

Once you have mastered the emotions, you can show just a bit of anger and say something like, "Nice hand. It takes a lot of courage to play cards like that." Or maybe you could simply ask out loud, "Let's see, now. What did you have on the flop? (Or what cards did you start out with?)" Those statements will allow some of your anger to burn off and it probably won't have an effect on the one who played them.

WARNING: Do not counter a stupid play with your own brand of stupidity!

21

Respect Your Opponent

You can ask almost anyone if they know how to play poker and they will answer yes. The reason they answer yes is that most people have played "kitchen table" or penny-ante stuff. The good player says to himself, "Wonderful." Correct? Of course, correct.

It reminds me of the story of the man who met an attractive woman and wanted to find out more about her. He asked, "Do you play the piano?" She replied, "Perhaps. I haven't tried it." As we all know, it takes a lot of practice to even be a novice at the piano.

How does that story apply to poker? It seems to me that most people who learn the general idea of poker feel they can play the game with almost anyone. Once they memorize which hands beat other hands (flush beats a straight, etc.), they see themselves as good to adequate players. That is why the good player says to himself, "Wonderful."

The good player needs those novice players, novice players who think they can play, to pay the freight. Those novice players present us with our best chance to show a profit.

PLAYER ABUSE

What overwhelms me is the following scenario, a scenario I have seen over and over again. A beginner player doesn't recognize that he is in a dangerous situation and calls all raises. Well, son-of-a-gun, he catches his magic card and beats the good player who was trying to get him out of the pot. Then the abuse starts. "How could you draw to only one card in the deck? Didn't you see that I had you badly beaten? What's the matter with you?" These and many other sarcastic statements are directed at the one who is stacking the chips.

WHY?

It is a mystery to me why the good player will turn on those novice players with verbal abuse. Those novice players are his bread and butter, his ticket to profit. Yet, in his anger, the good player seems to do his level best to drive the man away from the game. I recall a quote by Philo: "Be kind, for everyone you meet is fighting a hard battle."

It seems to me the player should go out of his or her way to accommodate the novice player. He should encourage each and every one of them to have fun playing poker. Talk to them, laugh with them, find out where they are from. I saw this kind of friendliness in action on my last trip to California. After a couple of hours, a man sat down in the empty seat and it was apparent he had not played much poker. Immediately the guy next to me engaged this man in conversation. The new man, Ed, was from Chicago and traveled to the Los Angeles area once or twice a month. He was well dressed, sold computer software for a living and had three kids. Frank, the man next to me, had lived in Illinois, and they had a great time all afternoon. Ed, needless to say, lost quite a few dollars, but left in an upbeat mode. He even said he would come back to play on his next trip to California. Frank took down some of Ed's money, but he made Ed feel good about playing. Respect for an opponent is an important concept to develop for your own sake and also for your wallet.

22

A Losing Streak (Part One)

A losing streak is about as much fun as getting soap in your eye or going in for a root canal. The facts of the case are that everyone gets soap in their eyes on occasion and every poker player will hit a losing streak. That is just the way the world turns, the way the cookie crumbles. When the losing streak comes on, my son's comment is applicable: "I think we are in deep yogurt."

Deep yogurt indeed. That peculiar transcendental divine being we call "the poker god" has some curious ways. He/she/it passes over such deserving folk like we'uns and blesses some quaint character who sits down for the first time at the green felt, pulls out $20 and asks how to play the game. This poker divinity seems to find perverse pleasure in arranging the cards so that this seedy looking fellow stacks row after row of chips and then asks in all innocence, "You fellows play in here all the time? I'll sure have to come back when I get back to town. Cash me in."

SURVIVING A LOSING STREAK

If we can agree that a losing streak is a given for the poker player, we can begin to think of some strategies that might be helpful. Let's think together about what might help the next time you encounter one of these horror situations.

A friend of mine called me from California to moan and groan about an appalling turn of the cards. His story was one of frustration. He would have by far the best hand going into the last card and, bingo, a strange card arrives and some nice lady about 81 years old would show him the mortal nuts. It wasn't a receding hairline that worried my friend, it was absolute baldness. His frustration was causing him to pull out his hair.

I tried to calm him down and when he was more rational, he agreed that he was letting the frustration get to him. He said, "After all, Andy, how many times does this have to happen before you lose your sanity? I lost over $500 in a $3-$6 game. That is the 14th time I have lost in the last 15 times I have played. What can I do?"

23

A Losing Streak (Part Two)

Yes, indeed. What can you do? Unfortunately, there are no easy answers. There are some schemes that might be helpful.

1. You *must* ask yourself the honest question, the significant question (and give an honest answer): "Is this really a losing streak or am I playing badly?" If you feel you are playing the best poker you can possibly play and have enough experience to know that you **should** generally win, then you could be in a genuine losing streak. What do your records say? Do you have a 90 percent loss record for the last month? Are you getting poor cards consistently? Are you having the second best hands time after time? (If you don't keep records — sorry, I have nothing to say to you.)

2. A losing streak will absolutely magnify any leaks you have in your play. Now is the time to take a vigilant look at all aspects of your game. Are you fudging just a bit on your starting hands? Are you staying to look at just one more card? Do you make "hope" calls? Do you get angry and tilt out when you get a bad beat?

If any of the answers to these questions are yes, you can tighten up and save yourself a bunch of money even if you are in a losing streak. These leaks are more evident during a bad run because you are taking in so few chips.

Steve was having a long stretch of "tough luck," as he called it. Since he depended on his poker playing to support him, he finally made the choice to completely re-examine his game. He first examined his choices of starting hands, then his betting strategies, his method of reading players and all the other factors that make up good poker playing.

After a diligent examination, he concluded he needed to make some drastic changes. He settled on a program he calls "aggressive folding." He has been testing this strategy for several weeks now and is reporting very good results. He is posting a win rate of over 85 percent. It is my opinion that a win rate of 85 percent in low-limit poker is a good rate.

At this point, Steve would say that he had some dramatic leaks in his game and that a losing streak helped him realize the need for an overhaul of his complete game. He was able to look past the pain of a losing streak and ask the significant question and change his style.

3. Another question you must ask and honestly answer is about your personal life. If you are having problems with the spouse or with the kids, take a holiday from the tables. Be careful not to play after you have been drinking. You need all of your ability to concentrate on poker, and anything that distracts you is big trouble. So during this time of poor cards, play only when you are in good emotional and physical shape.

24

Something Good Will Happen Eventually

"Oh, great poker god, give me patience and get it to me *real* soon!"

We all have it! Each and every man, woman and minor that ever sat behind a pile of poker chips has it. I have it. You have it. We have a disease, an addiction that costs us thousands and thousands. What is this disease, this addiction, you ask?

The horrible thing that costs us so much money is the *urge* to play. Maybe it is more accurate to say the *lust* to play. The desire to jump into the action of the game and gamble is what costs us thousands and thousands.

That urge costs most of us big bucks every year. For instance, we look at our first three cards (in Seven Card Stud) and find a pair of nines with a ten. Not a bad hand. But wait! That obnoxious smart aleck over there has a nine showing. And two people have tens in front of them. Now our hand is trash. It was a marginal hand, but playable in the right situation. This certainly is *not* the right situation. To put money in the pot, to gamble with that hand, would be dumb. To play that pair of nines in that situation would indicate you have the "urge" so deep in your bones that you might be incurable.

Here is a real-life illustration to demonstrate the "urge." I raised in early position with a pair of aces in a low-limit Texas Hold 'Em game. One of those know-it-all-type players had the button and he called with ace-three offsuit. You can figure how many outs this guy had! Just a couple of clicks to the left of none. The flop came K♠–8♠–3♣. That guy is now firmly attached to the pot. The first player to act makes a bet and I raise. The smart aleck calls and I'm hoping one of them doesn't have a K-8. The next card is the case ace, although I don't know it at the time. I bet and the smart aleck raises. The others drop and I re-raise. He calls. The last card is a three. When he raises me again, I am pretty sure what he has and he pays off big time. That "urge" to play can be down right ghastly. His threes full of aces doesn't get the job done against aces full of threes. Deep in my heart I chortled and knew this guy had the "urge" real bad.

PLAY GOOD CARDS

Everyone who plays low-limit poker knows that quite often a poor hand will draw out on the better hand. That is truth. Even when you have the best hand at the start there is no guarantee. The more marginal hands and trash hands that you have drawing at you, the less the chances of the best hands holding up. That is a fact of life in low-limit poker. However, keep playing only the best hands and, eventually, good things will happen. I am not saying it is always easy. We all know the frustrations of getting run down again and again by some clown who has no idea as to how the game should be played. Don't lose sight of the goal by playing like the guy who called my raise and lost with ace-three offsuit. Don't let the "urge" destroy your bankroll.

25

Patience And The Poker Player
(Part One)

Nothing separates me, a poker player, from profit more than the lack of patience. Nothing! Is that statement strong enough? When I sit down at a poker table I want to win. Otherwise, I would go to a movie, work out at the gym or watch women. Profit is my one and only motive. I want those dollars so that I can spend them for my own pleasure. I can think of no better reason to play. The one consistent and pervasive barrier that I must overcome to be a consistent winner is to be patient. If I can contain the powerful urge to play with hands that are usually losers, I will generally win. Like the knights of medieval days, we must be extremely careful about what weapons we choose to fight our battles.

STARTING HANDS

Let's talk about the practical application of patience to the games we play. The choosing of our starting hands is the worst culprit in profit prevention. My friend, Mike Caro, The Mad Genius, and a very wise man, writes that "inexperienced players enter too many pots." I agree completely and would go even one more step and say that *experienced* players enter too many pots.

I see so many players just giving their money away by playing low-quality and marginal hands. It appears they are not motivated to win as much. Why else would someone play A♦–Q♥–7♣ in Seven Card Stud? Or a Q-9 offsuit in early or middle position in Texas Hold 'Em? Those are dumb calls. If you play those hands 100 times, they will lose money. Sure, everyone gets lucky and will win with them, but they just cannot stand up over the long run. Give our special Lady Luck a break and play hands that have a chance to win money more often than lose. Wait until you get the potentially big hand.

Some of the results from these software packages are enlightening. If you have access to one or more of them, check out how often the most selective players win the fewest pots, but quite often win the most money. I saw one printout recently in which the patient player played only a few pots, but ended up in an eight-hour session with twenty times his buyin and most of the other players lost money. The loose players won *three times* as many pots, but still lost money. How do you explain that?

MONEY OR ACTION

The loose player had lots of action and if that was what he was looking for, great. Personally, I want profit. I want money. To me, money is better than action. The loose player just lets his money slip out of his hands, back into the game. The patient player waited for his best hands, invested his money and *won*. The loose player tried to make every hand a winner. No one can do that.

Remember, profit is the best reason to play poker.

26

Patience And The Poker Player
(Part Two)

Another profit depreciation factor is good starting hands that get run down and you continue to play them. It is unprofitable to ride a dead horse! I can understand the urge to play that pair of aces come hell and nut flushes, but they sure do suck up the money. There is something beautiful and compelling about those big pairs, but falling in love and getting married to them is bigamous. It is better to live the single, monogamous life and have money to spend on candlelight dinners, fast cars and charming women/men (as the case may be).

To me it is just criminal how people will play a pair of jacks (in Texas Hold 'Em) until the showdown when aces, kings and/or queens have hit the board and there is a bet and a raise. They just can't seem to give up on them. Maybe we overplay them because we get them so seldom and develop a sense of power when we catch them. When you have a big pair and it gets run down, abandon ship. Have the self-control to wait until you get them again and hope the circumstances are much better. Remember, there is nothing magic about big pairs. They often lose, and one should not be distressed. Be relentless in your ability to wait until they become the best hand. That stamina will be the difference between your play and how others play — or rather, *misplay* the big pairs. That stamina or patience will improve your profit picture.

The third part of this chapter is about being patient when you catch a long run of unplayable starting hands. After an hour of throwing back each and every hand, your nerves begin to wear thin. People are winning money and you have to sit on the sidelines and watch. It requires endurance to sit peacefully for an hour, two hours, three hours, however long it takes. The tenacity to sit waiting like the vulture is a virtue for the successful player. Fortunately, it is a virtue that can be *developed*. If we have the doggedness to just wait for those good hands to start coming again, and wait without complaint, we are well on our way to overcoming our opponents. Seldom will you see a poker player who has the fortitude to wait without complaint and anxiety. We can. We can be stoic. We can have the self-control to be unflustered by a dry spell. In fact, we expect the long dry spell and plan for it. We know it happens to everyone, and the dry spell becomes a challenge to see how long we can endure without becoming grouches. Patience to the good poker player becomes second nature. A second nature that wins for him.

There is a "hunger" to play a lot of poker hands. Every poker player has that hunger. We want to stack the chips, we want to "feel" like a winner. However, that hunger is often our downfall. Our ability to overcome that hunger will be directly proportionate to our winnings. The more times we err and enter pots with marginal hands or downright trash hands, the more times we expose ourselves to losing our chips. When we hold on to good hands that get run down or ride dead horses, we expose ourselves to losing our chips. The more times we become impatient with a long run of bad cards and start playing hands that are poor, we again expose ourselves to losing our chips. Give yourself more chances to succeed. Patience and the successful poker player are synonymous. Check it out.

TOURNAMENT PLAY

A truly wonderful event has happened in America and all around the planet. Low-Limit tournaments have become popular. Literally hundreds are played every week. Some are re-buy tournaments, some are shoot-outs, some are progressive, some are one table. For the low-limit player, tournaments are an incredible way to have some fun, accept a challenge and earn some great money.

Some poker players play a tournament like they are trying to kill snakes; they jump around like crazy. Some poker players play a tournament as if they were trying to commit suicide. Some poker players play a tournament exactly like they play live action. All of these approaches to tournament play are wrong. Why? Read the next eleven chapters to find out.

There are an incredible number of variations of tournaments. Study whichever type is current in your community. I believe you will discover some approaches to the particular modification that will vastly improve your chances of winning. Just the act of thinking about tournament play will put you way ahead of most of your competition.

27

Tournaments Are A Different Gig

The other day I played in a six-table Texas Hold 'Em tournament. The poker room people broke down the live action games and started the tournament. I swear over 60 percent of the players did not alter their style of play one bit (or one bet) from live action to tournament play. Obviously, they did not discern that live action and tournament demand dramatically different styles of play.

Let me illustrate: I saw one player defend his blind with a trash hand (7-4 offsuit) against a raise and two players who called the raise. I don't care what your chip situation is (his was about average), you have no business in that hand against some obviously good hands.

TOURNAMENT VERSUS LIVE ACTION

Your style of play in a tournament *should* be dramatically different than your play in live action. Why? There are two basic reasons:

1. You can play bad in live action, buy more chips and recover your loss with a lucky hand or two. In tournament play, you probably won't have the chance to come back and so you *have* to survive to get a payoff.

2. *The payoffs are different.* You have to end up at the final table to get a payday. The longer you survive, the higher you place, so the rewards are multiplied. First place often gets more than the combined totals of fourth, fifth, sixth, etc. Because the payoff is so top heavy, you must approach the game with a different style of play.

HIGHER PERCENTAGE OF LUCK

All tournaments are short term. That is a key fact. Any short-term poker session is strongly slanted for whoever has Lady Luck with them that day. That is an obvious statement. My purpose in stating it is that lots of poker players say a tournament is all luck, and that is definitely untrue. There is still a huge amount of skill required to win tournaments on a regular basis. You simply must adapt to the unique requirements of tournament play. Your regular live action play just won't get the job done as often as you will with a tournament modification.

A CHIP AND A CHAIR

The chip and chair concept is often overlooked by live action players when in a tournament. For instance, you make a raise with a good starting hand, say A♠–K♠ in Texas Hold 'Em and catch a flop like t♥–8♥–9♠. Suppose there are two callers before the flop, one of them the blind. The blind hand now bets out. You only have two chips left. Should you call? Most live action players would throw in their last two chips and hope for a miracle. Wrong. Save those chips for the next hand or the one after that. You still have a chance, slim though it may be. Maybe you will pick up a big pair. The fundamental fact of tournaments is survival. Many a player has gone on to win first place after he has been down to one chip. Open yourself up to luck as much as possible. With a flop like ten-eight-nine, you could be faced with a straight already made or perhaps two pairs. Maybe you could win if an ace flopped, but the blind might have an ace-ten. Abandon ship and survive.

28

The Big Difference

I have made a big deal out of the differences between the ways a good player will approach live action and tournament play. What are the major differences? How can you become proficient in both tournament and live action?

At this writing, little has been written about tournament play. This in itself is a marvel because there are so many tournaments being played all across the country. Could it be the other poker writers out there don't want to let anyone in on their secrets? Hmmmmm.

HAND SELECTION

Well, my secret is out now. One major way to improve your win ratio in tournament play is one of the basic ones, hand selection. What kind of hands should one select? In the early stages of play, my answer is to not play a draw hand. In Texas Hold 'Em, this means big pairs only. Usually just aces and kings, and sometimes queens. If the pot has not been raised, I will play and raise with queens. If the pot is raised in front of me, I will muck a pair of queens. If I have the aces or kings and the pot is raised in front of me, I will re-raise. After the flop, provided it isn't a real dangerous flop (three of a suit or ten-jack-queen), I will bet if it is checked to me. If I have the aces and it is bet into me after the flop, I will usually re-raise. The reason for doing so is that I want to define the hand at the lower betting limits.

In a Seven Card Stud tournament, I will only play trips, aces, kings and queens. I will raise with all of them unless I am behind a good player who has raised with a bigger door card than my pair. For instance, if I have queens and a good player raises with a king or an ace showing, I am done with it. Again, I will not play a draw hand like three parts of a flush or a straight. I certainly won't play three picture cards.

WHAT ABOUT A PAIR OF JACKS OR TENS?

What I will do with a pair of jacks or tens depends on the situation. If I am last (or next to last if the player on my left is a bit timid), I will raise with them, provided, of course, that the pot has not already been raised. If I get called, I will be very cautious. If any door card is paired, I will check. If an ace or king should fall, I will bet once and hope my opponents fold. Unless I improve those jacks or tens real quick, I don't want to invest any more money in them. Remember that the payoff in the tournament is not proportionate. Your medium-strength hands are suspect, so don't attempt to bet for value with them. Survival is the most important consideration. Play tough, tight and smart.

GET OUT EARLY

One bad carryover from live action play into early action of tournament play is continuing to play when you have marginally correct pot odds. Suppose you get caught is a situation where you are a slight favorite to catch the winning hand, but it will cost you some checks to call. Don't risk it. Get out early. Save those chips for a better situation when you are a much stronger favorite. This is a very important concept to remember as you switch from live action to tournament play. Survival is far more important than percentage play.

29

Raise Or Fold

There is a very old axiom in poker that has fundamental truth in it. I'm sure you have heard it. It simplifies some decisions that we are forced to make at the poker table. That axiom is "Raise or fold." That saying incorporates the concept that a person who consistently "calls" is a losing poker player. The axiom of raise or fold maintains you have either the best hand or you don't. If you don't have the best hand, get out. If you do have the best hand, raise. Simple, right? Oh, that it were that clear-cut and straight-forward. However, in tournament play, that axiom is very close to the correct philosophy to have.

NO DRAW HANDS IN THE TOURNAMENT

In the last chapter, I discussed some strategies regarding when not to play draw hands. Since tournament play payoffs are so top heavy, survival is more important than value betting. When you catch a draw hand in a tournament, it is usually best to throw it away. If you should decide to play it because of your position, your chip position and/or other factors, raise with it and put the pressure on the other players. Here is that concept in action: raise or drop. Even though you need players to make the pot odds necessary to justify playing the draw hand, the overriding factor is survival. You want that ante money, that blind money *now*.

Say you are in late position in the middle rounds of a Texas Hold 'Em tournament and you catch k♣–q♣. You are second or third in chip count, so you decide to play the hand. You raise with it and hope the players behind you get out and put the pressure on the blinds. The best thing is for all of them to fold and let you have the pot. Nevertheless, you are in a pretty fair situation if only the blinds call. Even if you don't catch on the flop, you have position on them, and if they check, you can bet and place their call in jeopardy. There is a danger you will run into trips or two pairs, but that is one of the risks.

In Seven Card Stud, suppose you catch a pair of tens in the pocket with an ace showing. You are next to last to act and you have a decent chip factor. If there is no other ten or ace showing, go ahead and put in a raise to see if you can collect the antes. You might have the best hand, or you might be drawing, but you should be okay unless you have some idiots in the game who will pursue any little pair and could run you down.

A starting hand you don't play in Seven Card Stud is three medium cards to a suit or three to a straight. Don't raise with those hands and hope to draw out. The odds are too long for comfort.

These "raise or fold" strategies are especially effective if you have not played any hands up to this point or defended your blinds with marginal hands. The observant players will have to put you on good hands and will lay down hands that might even beat yours. My system is to develop an image of extremely tight play and then use that image in the middle and late stages of the tournament to get people off better hands.

The raise or fold axiom will stand you in good stead in tournament play, but you will need to be very selective in your application. There is no way of knowing what kind of players you will have in your game. When you are up against players who have no idea of how a tournament should be played, you have to be extremely careful. They will not respect your raise and might get lucky and beat you. Beware.

30

Survival

When I was in my twenties, I got stuck in a prairie blizzard in western Minnesota. My car got stuck in a snow drift. I had about half a tank of gas, a couple of blankets, a candy bar and a candle. That was my total supply of survival equipment. The wind howled, the snow drifted higher and higher on the lee side of the car. After twelve hours it finally quit snowing. That was the good news. The bad news was that when it quit snowing, the temperature dropped dramatically. The wind continued to blow and the chill factor must have been close to forty below.

To survive, I would run the car for a few minutes to warm up and then shut if off to conserve gas. The candle provided some heat while it lasted. When the gas gauge got down to near empty, I tore up the backseat material and used it to wrap my feet and legs to help keep them warm. It was pretty scary.

Do you know what the worst part was? The worst part was fighting the urge to get out of the car and walk somewhere for help. I had to fight that craving constantly. To leave the car was almost certain death, but that yearning was always there.

Sometime during the second night, the wind quit. Then I ran out of gas and was just hanging on, trying to stay awake, knowing that if I fell asleep, I would freeze to death. Way out across the prairies, I saw a light. It was a snowplow working its way along the road. I was sure glad to crawl into that warm cab of the snow plow and get warm.

I tell this story to illustrate that survival is a matter to take seriously in a snow storm or in a poker tournament. In order to survive you have to resist the yearning to play marginal hands and risk your entire stack. Each and every hand you play is to risk your entire stack. Before you throw chips into the pot, consider that each hand you play is potentially your last. Ask yourself if those particular cards, your starting hand, is worth the risk of the entire tournament. In Texas Hold 'Em, say you catch ace-ten offsuit in middle position. Should you play? Ask yourself, "Is this hand worth the tournament?" In Seven Card Stud, you catch a pair of queens but a good player with a king showing raises in front of you. Should you play? Those ladies could cost you the tournament. You decide. Remember that urge I had in the middle of a snowstorm to leave the car and seek other shelter. You are risking everything. I was not in a very secure place in the automobile, but it was more safe than being out in a blizzard in which you couldn't see 50 feet in any direction. You think about those queens. You haven't caught a hand for an hour and those queens look really good. The temptation is real, make no mistake. It is those demons that we must fight if we want to win the tournament. It ain't easy.

My friend, Mike Caro, The Mad Genius, writes that we should look for good situations, not necessarily big cards. That pair of queens above, for instance, are good cards but in a bad situation. Throw those seductive ladies away and wait for a better chance. Even if you run out of gas or almost all your chips, hang on. Don't give up until *all* hope is gone. The payoff is big, either in life or a grand reward at the final table.

31

Don't Be A Loose Cannon

If you bust out of a tournament playing a very good hand, you have done well. If you bust out of a tournament playing a rag hand, shame on you.

From the first hand dealt to the last one you play, dedicate yourself to playing quality cards. Play nothing else. As you well know, I cannot sit here in front of my computer screen and tell you to play this hand and not that exact hand at every level of tournament play. I certainly recommend playing only the high pairs in the early going. However, when the blinds and antes go up, you should have developed a "feel" for the way the opposition is playing and devised a strategy for playing those critical middle rounds. You should have a good idea how the players on your left react to a raise. If they are pretty tight players who will lay down a hand, you can call and raise with certain marginal hands in some situations. If these players on your left are loose and lucky, you can only raise with the very best hands.

When I drew my seat in a Texas Hold 'Em tournament last week, AJ was on my immediate left and Gene was the third player over. Both AJ and Gene are excellent players. The man between them was a newcomer and I noticed he played about 60 percent of the hands. The cards he showed were pretty ragged and he had managed to win one big pot. By the middle rounds, after the color change, his stack was pretty small and he was tightening up. With this lineup on my left, I felt I had the green light to play some marginal hands when I had the button and the next two hands. Three out of ten spots to play aggressive is a pretty good ratio.

When the button got to me, I was looking at k♠–j♥ in my hand. It had not been raised, so I did the honors. AJ dropped, and the big blind called. The flop came q♥–t♣–4♦. Not at all to my liking, but not terrible. The blind hand checked and I bet. He called. My guess was he had a ten or maybe a j-9. The next card off was a jc. The blind checked and I bet. He threw his hand away. Whew!

During the next hand, with the button in front of AJ, I had a q♥–t♣. Again, it was not raised, so I made a stab at collecting the blinds. I knew AJ would either re-raise or drop and I hoped to just pick up the blinds. Sure enough, it worked. They all folded.

Please remember, this situation I just described was a very select situation. It is seldom you get that kind of perfect setting. With two out of three guys on my left being people who would respect a raise from me, I had the license to bet some marginal stuff. I could *never* have bet those hands in early or middle positions *or* against loose opposition. K-j and q-t offsuit are rag hands in anything but ideal situations.

Don't be caught up in the tournament action and lose perspective. In short, don't be a loose cannon. Play only quality stuff and have the motto, "Raise or Fold."

Ted Williams was one of the greatest hitters to come along in baseball. When he went to the plate, he went up there looking for "his pitch." If the pitcher served up that pitch, the odds were excellent that Williams would deliver a hit. He knew that his average would suffer if he went after pitches that were even slightly out of his best zone. So he restricted his swings to only those pitches that he felt were quality. Do the same in tournament play, and your winning percentage will go up dramatically!

32

Relax — Let The Cards Come To You

I find it an awesome temptation to "press the cards" in a poker tournament. In a tournament I want to establish a pattern of playing, a system of taking down pots so that I can win this thing. The urge to press the cards can be my demise. When I yield to these longings, usually I end up standing instead of sitting. I have developed a motto to help me counter these yearnings. That motto is: Relax, the cards will come.

This motto has evolved for me from two sources. Obviously, the first came because of playing in tournaments. The second source was a computer software game that I purchased from ICONWIN. As part of their Texas Hold 'Em software package, they included a regular tournament section and a one table freeze-out tournament section. Playing these programs has helped me determine that patience will pay off big time. Sure, there is one hell of a lot of difference between a computer-generated game and a game of real players. No sensible person will say that the computer can duplicate live players. However, there is much to be learned from a computer simulation. For one thing, you can get a lot of action packed into just a few moments. A computer will race to the end of each hand after you have dropped out. You can also learn to read the assigned values of the silicone opponents, which will help you put "fixes" on real players.

I found out from computer programs that there is a powerful urge to hurry up and enter the action. I found that I was pressing the hands, forcing the cards. Unfortunately, when you crowd the hands, you generally end up on the sidelines. When I learned to relax and wait for the best quality cards to come, I began to win with greater regularity. Sure, sometimes you can press the cards and get lucky. You see it every tournament: One guy plays marginal and trash hands that come in and he has a huge stack of checks. I have also noticed that those guys seldom win the tourney. They make their big move early and pile up a huge stack. Few of these players back off and play very selectively after their rush. If they could settle down and play quality cards, they would be ferocious competitors. Seldom do they make it past the middle rounds when the higher limits eat up their chips, and they seem puzzled that they can't pull down a pot with trash.

DON'T PRESS THE CARDS

Your chances of winning a tournament are greatly enhanced if you wait for the cards to come to you. Like a good racquet ball player, wait for the opportunity and then cash in. Wait for that ball to come to your strong side and then punish the opponent. In poker, wait for those quality cards and then come in with power. If you have any doubts about the quality of the cards in regard to position and quality of the opposition, don't take chances. If you have misgivings about the cards, throw them away. Play only with confidence and intensity. Hope hands or halfhearted play will seldom get you the pot. Play to win, and you will win.

33

Raising Hands Versus Calling Hands

I have already made it clear that tournament play is almost always a raise or drop situation, with a preference for the drop if you have any questions at all about the quality of your hand in that particular situation. Taking the lead from a few of the politicians of our time, I am covering my derriere with the word, "almost." Since it is probably wise to never say never, there are a few situations in which it is slightly better to call than to raise. Finding and using those situations to your benefit is not the easiest thing, but with experience, you will add another weapon to your arsenal. No one will quibble that a well-supplied arsenal is a valuable asset. The more weapons you have to confuse the opposition, the greater your win ratio. "Elementary, Dr. Watson?"

I am going to list two situations in which a call is appropriate, based on the relation of starting hands and position. Obviously there are more than two situations and more combinations of factors than just starting hands and position. However, this is just one chapter in a book that covers a whole bunch of things. I can't include everything. Sorry.

One situation in which you can use a call instead of a raise is to exploit an aggressive player. The most apparent circumstance is this: Suppose you catch a big pair in the blind and the aggressive player is on your right, on the button or just to the right of the button.

His usual tactic is to raise to drive out the blinds. You have maybe defended one or two blinds up to this point. So when this clown raises with you holding the big pair, you lick your lips in anticipation. You call, with say your pair of queens. The flop comes something like j♥–7♣–6♠. You pray he has a jack. You check and he bets. Again you call. He has to be suspicious now, but he can't give you a free card either. The next card is a 3♣ This time you check-raise him. If he indeed has a jack, he is trapped. He could not believe you call a raise with a 4-5, so you have him in for a lot of money.

The second situation in which to use the call is when you are in late position with a draw hand. This has to happen in either an early or middle round. Suppose you are in late position near the button, with no aggressive player yet to act. Two people call before it gets to you. You have a pair of eights. This time you call, hoping to catch an eight or a straight draw. This call does a couple of things for you. It gives you a cheap chance to catch an eight, and it plants the idea in the observant people's minds that you do more than raise or drop.

If you should catch an eight, you are in great shape. If you catch a flop where you are the over pair, you might be able to bet the hand and get out the draws. The danger of a low flop is that one of the blinds might have caught two pair or a straight. If so, they will check-raise. Be ready to abandon those eights if you get check-raised or called and then a lead bet after the turn card. Don't forget, those unimproved eights are not a powerful hand in a tournament. The whole purpose of calling with those eights was for a cheap chance to catch a big hand and to plant a false image. Do not invest much money in them.

Don't be too anxious to play draw hands except when you have a strong chip position and the table you are at has the correct image of your play, that is raise or drop.

34

Calling A Raise

A successful tournament player will have one thing firmly in mind. What is absolutely critical for mastery on the tournament trail is knowing which starting hands qualify for a raising hand and which hands qualify for calling/raising when someone else has raised. An outstanding player will have a clear image of which hands are which.

Let's look at a few examples to demonstrate my point. Suppose you are in a Texas Hold 'Em tournament. The blinds started at $5 and $10 and are $25 and $50 when you catch a king-jack offsuit. The button is three players to your left. What do you do? Well, I can't really answer what you would do, I might raise. I would make the bet $100 if no one had raised before the action got to me. My reasoning for raising is an attempt to drive out the players behind me, to try to force the blinds to fold and to create a situation in which I could win the pot whether or not I improved on the flop. Simple, straightforward tournament play, right? I don't have a great hand, but I might have the best hand at that moment. If I make an aggressive move, I stand a much better chance of winning the pot.

When I catch the king-jack offsuit in that situation, a simple call is the wrong move. I want to be the aggressor. I want to dictate the way that particular hand is played. I want to dominate the play of that hand.

If someone between me and the button should call me, I must make the assumption that this person has a viable hand. He might have a better hand. Not only could he have a better hand, he certainly has position on me. My situation is now perilous. I hope to improve on the flop, preferably with a jack as the high card. If I do not improve, I must calculate if I should risk another $50 to try to drive out the player.

Again, this is straightforward tournament play.

We have all seen it many times. Now, the same situation. I catch the same king-jack offsuit. This time the player to my right raises. Now what do you do? Do you call? No! A call is wrong! Wrong! The correct play is to fold.

Am I losing you? The same hand, the same position, and you should not even call? That king-jack is not a calling hand. What the player just told you with his raise (providing the player is an average sane individual) is that he has a good hand. That king-jack hand is a definite dog to the other player. Even if you have position on him, you should throw your hand away.

Let me illustrate. What if you call with that pig hand and catch a jack on the flop. The player bets out again. What do you do? Call? Raise? You have a problem because there is a chance the other player that raised has one of the big pairs. Suppose you catch a king on the flop and the other player bets out. You still have a problem because of your kicker. About the only hands you can beat is a pair of queens or a king-ten. Save your money for when you can control the action.

My point is that to be a good tournament player, you must be very clear as to what hands you can call a raise with and what hands you can raise with. Don't be fooled. Those cards look exactly the same, a king-jack looks just exactly like a king-jack. However, the circumstances are vastly different. One time you raise with it, another time you throw those losing cards away.

35

Get A Fix On The Players

Winning a tournament is the goal. Getting to the winners circle is the problem. How you get to that place where the payoffs happen takes work and skill. One of the skills I want to write about in this chapter is getting a fix on how the other players play the game. Anyone can get lucky and win a tournament. However, if you approach tournament play hoping for luck to pull it out for you, you will be at a disadvantage. Develop your skills and then luck has a better chance of finding you. As a salesman friend of mine would say, "The harder I work, the luckier I get." That is a true statement.

There will usually be no more than nine other players at your table. There will be fewer in Seven Card Stud. After two rounds, you should have a preliminary fix on each of those players! By a preliminary fix I mean you will have put each player into one of three categories: Complete novice, some knowledge of tournament play and good players.

NOVICE PLAY

Many players move from live action to tournament play with absolutely no change in their play. You need to identify each of those players! There is almost no use trying to put a move on a player who does not understand what he is doing. So you watch to see:

Do they understand the power of position?

Do they call with draw hands like 9-10 suited?

Do they use the philosophy of "raise or drop"?

Are they willing to use *muscle* or aggressive force when they have correct position?

Are they timid?

That is the first classification of players. If they don't have knowledge of basic tournament play, you must be more conservative against them. Now let's go on to the next level of play.

DO THEY ATTEMPT TO READ OTHER PLAYERS?

This is still quite an elementary level of tournament play. For this information, you usually watch their eyes to see how closely they follow the action. If you see what appears to be a mental recapitulation of the hand, they probably are at least at this level of play. If they request that a certain called hand be turned over, you can be quite certain they are trying to get a read on a player.

SOPHISTICATED AND/OR REAL EXPERTS

These last categories of players take a bit more refinement on your part if you want to distinguish between these players. Both of these types of players will be aggressive. They have learned that to win a tournament you must take some chances. Both levels of players will be adept at reading you and others. Both types of players will appear to be comfortable, patient and relaxed. Be very careful with these players. The real expert is by far the most dangerous because he is capable of reading you and makes an advanced move, either to fold a lesser hand or to make you lay down a better hand than he has. The real expert will make few mistakes in reading others. If you see that player lose a pot, you can move him down one category. This might be the only clue you will get between the player with some sophistication and the real expert.

36

The Guys Closest To You — On The Left

Winning play in a tournament demands a lot from each of us. In my last chapter I wrote about putting each player in a category as early as possible. There are some players at the table we must read with even greater scrutiny. These are the three players to the left and to the right. These are the guys or gals who will have the greatest impact on our won/lost record. These are the people we must work hardest on to find out how they play the tournament game. These players have the greatest impact on how we end up, one of the blowouts or one of the winners.

WINNING PLAY

I believe that to be a consistent winner in tournament play, you must have the courage to tackle a grizzly with a switch. You must also have the wisdom of Socrates, the bravado of Napoleon and the extra sensory perception of a mother. If you have those things going for you, hell, the rest is easy. However, since few of us have that combination of characteristics, we must work like a slave to achieve those tournament wins.

The most important people we need to work on to discover what level of play they are capable of on the particular day you encounter them, are the three people on your left. Those are the simpletons or experts who can do you the greatest damage. You must make a determination of their competence as quickly as humanly possible. For instance, questions like these must be asked: "Will any of them call a raise with a draw hand like 9-10 suited?" "Will any of them re-raise with a big pair?" "For God's sake, will one of them call a raise with a rag hand?" These are just a few of the many questions that should run through your head.

MODIFICATIONS

Once you discover how each one of those guys plays a tournament, you can make the adaptations necessary to compensate for the way they play. If you have one or more experts or sophisticated players, you can expect them to play only good hands. If one of them calls or raises you, you can expect them to have a good hand and can react appropriately. If you don't connect on the flop, simply save your chips.

If you have a couple of inexperienced players, it will be anybody's guess as to what they will call you with. The modifications you must make are to do less bluffing and play only solid hands against them when they call you.

Against the inexperienced players, it is also easier to set up a trap for them. When you get the right situation and catch the flop that hits you big and gives the sucker a bit less, you can have some fun. A huge part of the trap scenario is reading the player to ascertain if he or she is aggressive. If that person is a calling station and will not bet out unless they have the pure unadulterated nuts, it is impossible to trap them. When you find one of the timid ones, it might be best to just check and show the hand down with no more investment. If you know they will call you and never bet, unless you have a good to very good hand, just show the hand down.

37

The Guys Closest To You — On The Right

In the last chapter I wrote about the rotten scoundrels who happened to sit on your left. Those reprobates will try to take your chips from you and will be happy if you should go broke and be watching from the rail. Well, I have more bad news: The guys sitting on your right are of the same ilk. They want to take your chips just as badly as those unprincipled degenerates on your left. This means we must take appropriate measures to counter their unscrupulous efforts to deprive us of our checkers. (We, of course, will seek to divest them of their chips, but that is okay since we are honorable folks.)

Those guys and gals to your right are quite a bit less dangerous in the overall scope of things than the people on your left. Those citizens must act before you. You have the advantage of seeing their action before you are called on. Notwithstanding the obvious advantage you have of being able to act after they do, they will have a great impact on your success or failure in tournament play.

Once again you need to answer some basic questions about them. Questions like, "What do these guys raise with?", "What kinds of hands do they call with?" and "How do they react to a raise from behind them?"

Just the other day I was seated just to the left of a guy who was very aggressive in the early rounds of a tournament. When he raised the first few times, I just mucked my hand.

I didn't have much and certainly didn't want to expose my checkers to some guy who was red hot. After I saw the kinds of hands he was raising on, I changed my play. He was presenting me with a great opportunity! He would raise with any pair regardless of size. He would also raise with any ace and any two cards, ten and above. I started to drool. The next time he raised, I had a king and queen of hearts. That is not a great hand, but I put in another raise. He jumped a bit when I did it and favored me with a scowl. My re-raise forced the rest of the table to drop out and so I was heads up with this guy. This was exactly what I wanted. Unless he caught real good on the flop, his chips would be in my stack. The flop came j♥–7♥–2♣. He bet and I raised. He threw his hand away. I had nothing on the flop except a draw and the tremendous advantage of position. A few hands later he raised again when I had a fair hand, and I gave him another lesson on tournament manners. He was now running short of chips, so he modified his play and came in with only top-quality hands.

My point is not that I am some kind of genius when it comes to tournament strategy, but rather that we must take advantage of the way people play. To take this advantage, we must define their play. We must get a grasp of their poker values. We must find their weaknesses and capitalize on those weaknesses.

I watched a friend of mine get to the last few tables in a big tournament, and a guy on his right would not lay down a hand. This guy would call with a draw hand and when George would put in a raise, the guy would pay the price to show the hand down. This took away the benefit of bluffing from a superior position, and George simply changed his play. Unless George had a good hand after the flop, he would simply check. Knowing the man would call with any kind of hand, George quit trying to blow him off the pot.

Getting a fix on players on your immediate right will help you modify your play to maximize your wins and minimize your losses.

38

Trapping

Once in a great while it happens. These are rare circumstances, but when you pull one off, the feeling is fantastic. Rare as they may be, you can go for weeks of steady tournament play and not find the perfect opening, or you can sometimes find two in a row. I am talking about the trap. That glorious moment when you pull off the perfect play and everyone at the table silently applauds your action. The hushed admiration is stimulating. For a few moments, you bask in the glow of making a perfectly timed play that took down an opponent and embellished your stack and your table image. Ah! The glory of it all.

CHOOSING THE VICTIM

The trap is a powerful tool in tournament play. When it happens, the victim is usually taken out of the tournament completely or for all practical purposes so short of chips he or she will not be a factor. However, be aware that some opponents are so good that the trapper becomes the trappee. So beware the expert. He might put your trap hand where the sun does not shine.

BE OPEN TO THE OPPORTUNITY

Let us assume that we are all above average tournament players and consequently are always on the lookout for the perfect situation where we can pull off the trap. In order to pull off the ambush, we must carefully identify the potential trappee. He/she cannot be that timid mouse over in seat four. He/she must be an aggressive tournament player, willing to risk his/her chips. He/she is ready, willing and able to try to buy a pot, to try to steal the chips from their own mother. However, if you feel the potential pigeon is an expert player, be *very* cautious. That pigeon could turn into a vulture who will pick your bones clean.

Visualize how a big cat stalks its prey. He chooses his victim and watches. Without movement or sound, he sets the perfect way to bring it down. The cat is sneaky, silent, serene and has the heart of a killer. He doesn't move a muscle until the precise moment and with the ferocity of a tornado, he takes down the prey. With awesome quickness, with improbable power, with clear definition, the cat springs the trap and will eat for days on his victim.

That is a perfect picture as to how you will operate in your next tournament. You will be the master of the jungle, the lord of the hunt. And you will feast for days upon the remains of your victim. Oh, how glorious is the victory, how fulfilling is the reward. Others will speak of your mastery; the reporters will write about the play that won the tournament. You will smile humbly and accept the prize and use the money for absolutely licentious enjoyment.

Tournament play is extremely demanding. You must have the patience of a turtle, the judgment of a seer, the heart of an assassin, the dedication of a missionary. You have to be able to shut out all of the other parts of your life and focus on the task at hand. All of the weapons of your arsenal must be polished and sharpened. You must be impervious to danger and small wounds. You have come to the table for only one purpose, to annihilate the pedestrians who happen to compete for your pots. Do all of this and you will be the victor. May the poker gods and goddesses show you favor!

STRATEGY

I doubt that you throw dollar bills out the window of your car. Why would you throw away money at the poker table?

Strategy should take place at a number of levels: when you take time to think about the game (Planning), final review as you drive to the game, developing a strategy for starting hands, generating a style of play once the hand begins, reflecting on your play as you drive home.

Effective strategy includes knowing your numbers. What are the odds against making a flush draw after you have four parts? How often will you be dealt rolled-up trips in Seven Card Stud? What are the odds that you will flop top pair if you have an ace-king in your hand in Texas Hold 'Em? I'm sure we have all heard the wag say that his chances of catching his flush is fifty-fifty. Either he does or he doesn't. You should have a bit more definition than that.

39

Playing Low-Percentage Hands

Poker is an incredibly fascinating game. I attribute part of this fascination we have for poker to the luck factor. The luck factor in poker is widely accepted by many players as being *the* substantial element in winning. And luck truly is important, in the short run. Time after time a grass-green novice will defeat an expert. Why? Because of luck.

There is no doubt whatsoever that the expert will prevail over the course of several weeks. The expert is able to win more because skill plus luck will eventually defeat luck alone. Lady Luck will, in time, visit everyone. She does not discriminate. (It sure feels like it sometimes.) The novice will get his share of luck; the expert will get his share.

One important factor that often defeats the novice is his choice of starting hands. All too often he will choose a low-percentage hand when it appears there are strong (high-percentage) out against him. He chooses to do this because he *hopes* his luck will pull him through. For instance, a player in Seven Card Stud is dealt a pair of tens, and a good player with a king showing raises and another player with an ace showing calls. Those tens have no business competing in the pot! Sure, that player can catch another ten. However, the raiser has *exactly* the same chance to catch another king (assuming no king *or* ten has appeared). If you both catch the trip card, the kings win. If you both improve and catch an underpair, the kings win. If neither improve, the kings

87

win. Your opponent's chances of winning are a *lot* better than yours.

I was playing in a Hold 'Em tournament recently. I was dealt a pair of queens in fourth position. I raised and Macho called with a 6-8 offsuit. Against a raise, a 6-8 offsuit is a real dog hand. Macho was "hoping" his luck would get the job done. The flop came 7♠–7♥–4♦ with four players competing. I bet and Macho called; the others folded. A jack came on the turn, I bet and Macho called. A five came on the river and I lost the hand to his straight. By the way, one of Macho's traits is that he will pay almost any price to "snap off" a good player. Even though Macho won the hand, I love to have him in the game because he will play trash like that 6-8 offsuit in terrible situations. Sure, he will win once in a while, which is just exactly what I want to happen. He feels like he has conquered the world, and I want him in there drawing to those trash hands.

Playing a 6-8 offsuit is a perfect example of a low-percentage hand that uses the luck factor to win. Macho had a long-shot inside straight draw on the flop and paid his money to see a five. I can't complain, especially since Macho washed out of the tournament and I won it. The more often we can make the best play and have the best percentage chance to win, the more often we will win.

In Seven Card Stud, we consistently see people play small pairs against bigger pairs. In Hold 'Em, we consistently see people play ace-anything (offsuit and suited) even in early positions or after a raise. If you do that in Hold 'Em, ask yourself what you hope to hit on the flop. Certainly you don't want an ace nor do you want to pair your kicker. If you pair your ace, you have a huge kicker problem. If you pair, say, a six, any old overpair will beat you bad. The most logical "hope" is to catch two pair, aces over. Even then you can lose to two higher pair. Remember that "hoping" to hit two pair is about a 2 percent shot!

Holding low-percentage hands just doesn't make sense! Give Lady Luck a break and stick to good hands. You will be richer for it.

40

Know Your Game

A very big danger in my usual game is overplaying the players. I can just hear you say, "Come on, Andy, what does it mean to overplay the players?" I think I can best describe it by telling you first of all about the game I usually sit down in.

My "usual game" describes the general structure and makeup of the players here in the mountain towns of Colorado. One major factor determines much of how these games evolve. That factor is the $5 limit allowed by the state of Colorado. The maximum that each bet can be is $5. That $5 factor simply means that you can seldom drive anyone off the pot with your money. Only a few of the players can be influenced by a raise; a few more can be influenced by a re-raise. This is low-limit poker at its best.

One of my big themes is to channel the way you play so that you can maximize your wins based on the particular game you are usually in. Some of you play only home games in which the players are well known to each other. This allows you to keep a good record or book on each player. You get to know their tendencies or their lack of tendencies.

Some readers play in card rooms of various size. Some clubs have two tables, some have over a hundred. Playing in a club presents additional challenges to modifying your style of play to maximize your wins. The challenges come about because the makeup of the table will fluctuate from day to day, hour to hour. However, you can still draw some general conclusions about "your game". These conclusions are critical for profit.

In my game, the action is almost always wild. Therefore I design my play to take the fullest advantage of this wildness. I seldom enter pots with draw hands from early position. In Texas Hold 'Em, I will be extremely careful with the big pairs, dropping out early if the flop is dangerous. This sort of thing.

My weakness I have discovered in these wild action games is that I tend to give the players too much credit.

41

To Raise Or Not To Raise?

Many times I and other writers of poker tales and woes will write about certain axioms of poker. One axiom that I am fond of is the old phrase that goes something like "Either raise or fold. Only losers call."

I am surprised how often my students are confused about this concept. It seems to me that when a person is just learning to play poker, he or she is quite tentative. It is instinctive to be tentative. Until we know what we are doing, it is difficult to be aggressive and decisive. So it is with beginning poker players. They have a notion they should raise with a big pair but feel that it would be better to just call. When I ask them why, they will reply, "Well, it seems safer when I don't invest that extra money." I try to explain to them that just calling is allowing, yes, inviting even, some marginal and trash hands to come in cheap and draw out on them. They usually nod their heads and say, "Okay," and the next time they catch a big pair, they call again.

When their hand is exposed, they will look up at me, expecting to get frowned at and chastised. So I just shake my head, hoping they will eventually learn to become aggressive.

A MODIFICATION TO THE AXIOM

There is an important modification to the stated axiom of raise or fold. Quite often you find yourself in a drawing situation in which you have almost the correct pot odds to call, and if you raise, you could drive out the players you need to make the call a profitable risk.

The same is true for a flush draw or a high straight draw in Seven Card Stud. You have a long way to go to make your hand, so a call is better than a raise. If you should catch the card you need on fourth street, go ahead and bet it hard, depending on your position and table image.

Suppose you are in a low-limit Texas Hold 'Em game in fairly late position. You check your hole cards and find A♦–4♦. Not a great hand but certainly worth drawing because four people are already in the pot, including the blinds. A raise will certainly be acceptable, but a raise might drive out some good customers behind you as well as the blinds. At least some of the time a call seems like the appropriate response. On the flop you want either a straight, a flush, two pairs, or a draw.

These are certainly exceptions to the axiom. However, every time a person just calls with one of the big pairs in early position in Texas Hold 'Em, I mentally say thank you! I appreciate a cheap chance to draw out on you and ram those things where they belong if you don't put in a raise. Slow playing big pairs in low-limit poker is either dumb or unbalanced. That pair of aces gets beat often enough without encouraging callers. Some people will even slow play a pair of queens in early position, hoping someone will raise and then they can re-raise. God bless them, I say. They are just asking someone to beat them with an ace-six when an ace comes on the flop. Or a king with a bad kicker.

There are times you want to limit the field of players and times when you want lots of folks putting their money in the pot. Know which hands are which and don't be afraid to raise it up if you want to get rid of some of the draw-out artists.

42

Max Out Your Good Hands

Let's suppose you hit a big hand from middle position. Ask yourself, "How can I win the most money with this hand?" Here is a real-life situation:

In late middle position in a low-limit game of Texas Hold 'Em, you hold the ace-nine of diamonds. There are eight players in the hand. The flop comes with one of those long-shot hands (approximately 119 to 1) of three diamonds, 7♦–t♦–J♦. You have flopped the best possible hand because no one could have a straight flush.

The best part of this particular hand was that the first player to act has flopped a straight and he bets out. In low-limit games, players quite often do not respect or fear a flop with three cards of a suit. You have the mortal nuts and unless the board pairs, you cannot get beat.

THE QUESTION IN YOUR HEAD IS, "HOW CAN I MAX OUT THIS HAND?"

There are two callers before it gets to you and there are four players behind you. I believe it is best to not reveal the strength of your hand at this point. When I play, I want to see how the players behind me react. Since this is low-limit poker, a lot of players will even draw to pick up a draw. In this case you want them to all call in hopes of catching a draw. In some cases a low-limit player will hold a single diamond and draw in hopes of catching a fourth diamond on the board. If you raise at this point, you could well force other players to throw away their hands. You want them all to put their money in and draw.

THE BEST CARD

Probably the best card for you to catch is a nine or eight of another suit. That might give one of the players a straight and assure you of a call on the river. Also a king or an ace would be good cards.

This exact situation happened to me once where I flopped the nuts with little danger of getting hurt. There were four loose players behind me and so I did not raise on the flop. The turn card was a queen and again the first player to act bet out. He was called twice before it got to me, so I just called. Three people called behind me. A perfect situation. The last card was a deuce, and the first person bet out and was called twice before it got to me. Again, I smooth-called and two people behind me called. I sincerely doubt that I could have made any more money by raising.

The important thing to remember is that when you have the winning hand, try to max out the pot. You can't be right all the time — no one is. Once in a while a person will hit two runners and beat you, but if you have a feel for those players behind you, try to coax a call from them. Make them play for the long shots and you will reap the benefits. Don't be confused with the other times when you raise to drive people out of the pot. It is very critical for you to know when to raise to reduce the competition (see Chapter 40) and when to not raise to induce a call.

43

Coping With A Win Streak

Much has been written about how to cope with a losing streak. I have addressed the losing streak issue in several chapters in other books. A synopsis of those chapters is that the inevitable losing streak is the time to tighten up your game, stop the leaks, review your starting hand requirements and lower your win expectations.

Coping with a run of good cards is also a matter for serious reflection. This is the time to really have fun and enjoy this erratic game we call poker. It is also the time to maximize your win potential and log some big numbers to offset the times when the cards do not run like you think they should. Life at the poker table is often frustrating, so when the cards turn in your direction, enjoy and optimize this delightful event.

Let's compare some ideas on how to maximize the win potential during a good run of cards. First of all, we must be quite sure that a win streak is happening. I am not talking about a "rush." I define a rush as a set of circumstances where you win quite a number of hands within a short time frame, like an hour. We all get on rushes that usually last only a few moments. A win streak, by my definition, is winning several days in a row. It is logging a consistent win record of at least four out of five playing sessions.

The next thing I try to do when I sense I am pulling good cards that are winning is to expand slightly my starting hand requirements. Early on, this is just a test. For instance, in Texas Hold 'Em, in a loose game I might play a ten-jack unsuited in early middle position. Normally that is a muck hand for me. I would *not* play a pair of queens in Seven Card Stud after a good player raises with a king or ace showing. That is a stupid play, even when running hot.

In general I would loosen up my playing style. When normally I would call, I would consider raising. When raised, I would consider re-raising. If faced with a close situation in which I could either throw my hand away or call, I would call. I would do what a friend of mine says to do: "Give those cards a chance."

A warning: *Don't get crazy!* I believe a sure way to kill a win streak is to believe that no one can beat you. That little lady there in the mink stole will not be aware that you are hot. She will call your finest move and show you the winner, a pair of deuces that takes down your bluff. When I say loosen up, I don't mean get loose. Open up your style a bit and play a tad more aggressive, but don't assume that you can win just any old hand you want. In low-limit poker, you generally must show down the best cards. No one can expect to push through a trash hand whenever they think they should win. Keep that win streak alive with quality play and quality cards for the most part. Play a few more marginal hands than normal, but unless you are sizzling hot, be selective as to where and when you play borderline hands.

MOST OF ALL, ENJOY

My last word on this subject is simple. Rejoice in this wonderful experience of catching good cards. It truly is fun. Stand back and admire how this wonderful game plays itself out. You are now on top. Savor the moment.

44

Get Out Early

It is a given that we all love to contend for the money in the pot. We love the action. We relish the chance to compete. Each and every one of us has the desire to challenge the other players and win the money. Because of that craving, we need to compensate so that we do not do foolish things. By foolish things I mean entering the action when we are the underdog, when someone else is the favorite. Sure, we might win sometimes, but when you go uphill too often, I guarantee, you will lose. Save money by getting out early.

CHOOSING THE BEST STARTING HANDS

Picking your starting hands is of course, the best insurance for profit. Each hand is like a short distance race. The person with the best start is the favorite to win the race. So if you start with the best hand, your chances of winning are the best. However, let's move beyond the initial starting hand to the next betting round.

EACH BETTING ROUND IS A DECISION POINT

All of the traditional flop games (Texas Hold 'Em, Omaha, Pineapple) have four betting rounds. Seven Card Stud has five. The draw games have two. Since draw poker has only two betting rounds, the opening betting round and the final betting round, we will not offer any examples from draw.

Seven Card Stud, with five betting rounds, is the best game to illustrate my concept. Suppose you start and raise with two kings. Three people call you, one with an ace showing. On the next round you catch a nothing card and the person with the ace catches another ace. He bets and you get out. This is a simple case. When beat, get out.

Let's take a more complex case. You start with three hearts, again in Seven Card Stud. You catch a heart on the next card, so your hand looks like this: k♥–7♥–6♥–t♥. You have counted four hearts that are active or have folded, one of them the ace of hearts. Another person has X-X-A♣-t♣ showing and you have seen only one other club. *You might have an expensive problem on your hands.*

I suggest you play the hand aggressively at this point only to see if you can get a clue from the person with two clubs showing. By aggressive, I mean bet and raise as much as possible. If he catches another club and bets and you do not catch a heart, fold your hand. Even if you do catch a heart, it is probably still best to get out, depending on your evaluation of the player's skill. You are now on fifth street where the limits double if you are in a structured game. You could easily be drawing dead and be paying a big price to find out that you are second best.

My reasons for telling you to do this are:

1. The ace of hearts is gone. You cannot match or beat his flush, if he has one.

2. The limits have doubled and the price is high.

3. There is still a danger of someone catching a full house and beating you both.

4. It makes good economic sense to just retire and wait for a better opportunity.

45

Information Is The Winner

Last week I sat down in a low-limit Texas Hold 'Em game and the very first hand was a pair of tens in the pocket. I raised to help define the hand and get out some of the rag players behind me. Well, dag-nabbed flop came 10♥–6♣–2♠. What a deal. Top set and no terribly dangerous draws. I couldn't quite believe my good fortune. It was checked to me and I bet, confident that the usual low-limit players in our town will draw for a draw and there is no valid reason to slow play in the usual games. I was correct, five callers! I loved it. The next card off was a queen. Again I bet and got two callers. The last card was another deuce. This time I again got two callers, both with a queen in their hands. With a start like that, I cashed out a nice profit.

There are a couple of lessons to be learned from that scenario. One lesson is that this kind of winning hand and flop happen so seldom that you should thank the poker deities. The other lesson is that unless you hit a real big hand in the first 30 to 45 minutes, don't play.

Please note that in the above account of a winning hand, I made reference to guesses that I made, guesses that just happened to be accurate. I made some general assumptions that were based on earlier observations of other games but did not necessarily mean they would be true for this lineup. In other words, I lucked out.

Don't depend on luck like this for a marginal hand or even a decent hand in poor position. When you enter a poker game, take a few rounds to get a fix on which players are there and something about their play. Even if you know the player, you need to determine how that player is feeling today and what he is likely to do. *Information is a key to winning.* You need some basis of information before you take any chances. Sure, if you hit a big hand, play it out, but don't get out on a limb so that someone with a chain saw will cut off behind you. Be content with modest action if the board suddenly turns menacing. Don't push the betting until you have some more information.

The key reason for this is the loss limit that all of us place on ourselves. If we get forced into hand after hand of losses from the get-go, we could easily lose our money for the day and not even have a chance to make a score. Gather and glean information before you take any risks.

I realize the more astute players who play with you on a regular basis will observe this tendency and raise you out of pots that you might have a shot at winning. Don't fret it. Your time will come. Besides, those kinds of astute players are few and far between at the low-limit tables.

The first order of business for a good poker player is to get a "line" on each opponent. Even after an hour, you may only have an infinitesimal amount of information, but you will at least have lumped most of the players into the bigger categories. — who plays every hand, who plays once every two rounds, who slow plays the big pairs, etc. Your goal is to begin a slow process of bleeding money from each player into your stack. For centuries, the medical person in the community was known as "the leech" because he tried to cure patients by bleeding them. Think of yourself as "The leech." You are the one who will suck their money from them and use it for a good cause — your car payment.

46

Catch A Star

The health club I belong to has a few racquetball courts. I have played the game quite a few times and so have some understanding of the strategy and moves. A new young man came to the club one day and was a novice racquetball player. A few weeks went by, and I noticed that "Ted" had moved up from the novice list to the "B" list. Then I saw him just a couple of months later, Ted had moved up again. This time to the "A" list. When I saw him in the locker room, I asked him about his quick progress. He had a simple explanation: "All I did was to learn to wait for the ball to come to me. When I first started, I rushed the ball. Now I wait and I catch the moment. It works for me."

BELIEVE AND THEY WILL COME

What Ted said is a most important message for poker players as well. "Wait, and I will catch the moment." I have been horribly guilty of "rushing" the cards. I tried hard to make a hand work. When I caught a medium strength hand, I played regardless of position and chances of success. I often called a raise with mediocre hands because I had already called the initial bet.

Here is an illustration: Suppose I called with a pair of split sevens in a Seven Card Stud game. Another player, a good player, raised with a king showing and another player with an ace called. I knew I should have thrown those blasted sevens away, but no, I called the raise hoping to trip up. I was beat, knew I was beat and I still called. That is dumb and that is "rushing" the cards. Those sevens were a definite dog to the player with the kings.

One important fact that we cannot overlook is that good cards will come our way. "Sure," you say. "And the cow jumps over the moon." "Just wait and wait and ante our money away. And then everyone will call us a rock player and won't pay us off when we do catch." There is just enough truth in that statement to keep a myth alive. Action gets action, no one can deny. However, it is truly possible to overcome the "rock" label. However, undoing the "rock" label is beyond the scope of this chapter. This section is about developing the ability to wait until the cards come our way. When the cards do come, the time has come to have some fun.

BE SELECTIVE OF HANDS TO PLAY

We can "move up" the list just like Ted did. We can move from novice, beginner, intermediate and advanced into the expert class. We really can. One important lesson to log into our heads is what Ted learned: wait and catch the star when it comes our way. Trying to push the cards, to speed around, to force our way into winning the pot is costly.

This does not mean that we should be passive, by no means! When the cards come, when the star passes our way, *hit it*! Hit it and hit it hard. Raise and hammer. Push and shove. Elbow and claw. The difference is knowing when to make the big move. Wait for your moment in the sun and slay the dragons. You will be awesome.

47

What To Do When You Have An Early Loss

Why does it happen so often? Soon after I sit down, I catch good cards in good position and get them beat. Right off, I lose. And I lose the second hand I play. And the third. Ouch. Gosh darn it.

I get up and walk around my chair. I go to the bathroom and comb my hair. All this time I am asking myself, "What am I doing wrong? Did the poker goddess investigate my love life and is punishing me? Did I forget to put on deodorant? What iniquity did I commit?"

This scenario happens to me more than I care to remember. I get into a game and get stuck big time before I pull down a pot. That isn't supposed to be the case. Right? How can they do that to me?

This kind of loss happens, and we need to be prepared to handle the emotional reaction we have. That is the critical point. We *must* be able to control our losses and our emotions or we will end up doing major damage to the old bankroll.

HOW TO FIX AN EARLY LOSS

My first rule for myself is: "Don't panic." I talk quietly to myself to keep my emotions straight up. No tilt allowed! Tilt is a critical emergency that requires first aid, maybe even treatment in the intensive care unit. If I start to tip, drastic remedial action is required.

Therefore my first course of action is tilt prevention. My head must be clear and my intelligence must lead my emotions. If my emotions lead, I know I will lose.

DAMAGE CONTROL

My second line of thought is to institute damage control. It is entirely possible that I will continue to lose with good cards. Therefore it is imperative that I only play premium hands and be very conscious of position. The only time I can invest in a marginal hand is when the cost is minimal and I cannot be raised. At this point I cannot risk much money on a chancy situation. Remember that like General Custer at the Little Big Horn, you are surrounded by hostiles. Those hostiles will gladly take your scalp.

A third thing to recall is that this early loss syndrome creates a fear, a fear that could easily affect the way we play. Since none of us like pain and losing is painful, we could be very reserved in our betting approach. This kind of reservation can be appropriate under the circumstances. However, remember that being reticent in a poker game is not a moneymaking tactic in the long run. Realistically, fear has to be a factor. Don't overlook its impact.

The fourth reaction to an early loss is to tell yourself that the cards will eventually take care of you. That is, the cards will be your friends *if* you know how to cooperate with them. Do not, repeat, *do not*, try to get your chips back quickly. Plan on a program that will take several hours. Sure, you can get lucky and catch some big pots, but the usual situation is that you will have to claw and elbow your way back to even and into the plus column.

Early losses are a bummer. However, don't let the loss get you in a funk so that you lose even more money.

48

Putting Another Player On A Hand

Low-limit poker is a wonderful and popular institution. The number of low-limit players compared to the number of high-limit players is huge. Even the percentage of middle-limit ($10-$20 and up) poker players is low in comparison to low-limit. Most poker players are recreation players and, hence, they don't really want to invest a lot of time in in-depth study of the game. They just want to play, and low-limit is where they congregate.

You have probably looked at the heading just above this paragraph and said something like, "Wow, Andy is truly on his game today." It certainly does not take a brain surgeon to know the problems of reading low-limit poker players. At any limit in poker, accurately putting players on a hand is challenging. In low-limit poker, the chore of reading players is massive. I have made monumental errors. People have shown me hands that I not only missed reading completely, but I haven't even been in the same galaxy. When I replay the hand in my head, I am totally mystified as to how they could have even been in the hand, much less have called a raise or two.

My problem, it appears to me now after much reflection, is that I try to bring rational thought to the process of reading hands. The predicament is amplified because the rational process works often enough to confuse me. On the other hand, using only an irrational thought process, doesn't work well, either. So I am caught in the middle. Neither process can be used to dsthe exclusion of the other. They both will work under certain circumstances. The skill is knowing when to use the rational process and when to use the irrational. Are we having fun yet?

There is no doubt that the best way to improve your skills at reading the low-limit player is to practice the art at every hand. It is so much easier to keep a clear head and make better decisions when you are not involved in a hand. The goal we have is to practice enough while on the sidelines so that we are proficient in hand reading while embroiled in contending for the pot. We all know it is much more difficult to read players while we are in the hand because we are also concerned about a number of other factors. For instance, when competing for the pot we think about:

A. The relative strength of our hand versus that of our opponents. Is our hand strong enough to develop strategies to maximize our win potential or are we just hoping to get the hand shown down as cheaply as possible? Should we try to get people to drop or should we try to keep them in to contribute to the pot size?

B. We must determine who is on a made hand, who is on a typical draw like a straight or flush draw, and who is drawing at a second, third or under pair. Low-limit poker provides an abundance of possibilities.

C. We have emotional involvements. We must be aware of other players trying to hammer us, aware of our wishes to hammer someone and therefore make some unwise investments. We can have concerns about our bankroll, what the wife is cooking for dinner, a kid who is squandering our money at college, etc.

49

Stay Awake

Do you find it hard to concentrate on the play after you throw your hand away? If so, let me make a pitch for you to find the profit potential in watching the action when you are not involved.

To set the stage for my recommendation, I looked up "analysis" in my ninth edition of the Merriam Webster's Collegiate Dictionary. Here is what it said:

analysis: 1. separation of the whole into its component parts 2. an examination of a complex, its elements, and their relations.

Observation Equals More Money To Take Home (O=MMTTH)

I am in hopes that you bought this book so that you could take more money home with you after you read this material. I believe astute players learn from each other and you, the reader, hope to learn what some other soul has learned and is willing to share with the general public. If my reasoning is correct, O=MMTTH makes sense to you because you are willing to put a bit of effort into learning how this game of poker is played.

I doubt that hardly any clever players will question that the better way to learn about players is to follow what they do when they are playing a hand. That is, the analysis of the player. This analysis, I submit, is better done when one is not involved in the action. Since a good, solid player is not involved in the majority of the hands, he/she will have ample opportunity to observe and analyze. I promise that if you faithfully watch each and every player as they participate in the action, you will find it much, much easier to put them on a hand.

Each and every player in a hand will be giving you some clues as to the strength of his/her hand. Learning how to interpret those clues is vital to O=MMTTH. For instance, I played with a guy who would not raise with small and medium pairs in the pocket (Texas Hold 'em), but would re-raise with them if it was raised behind him. When I discovered that bit of information, he paid a dear price for his strategy.

The usual clues to watch for are how well the player watches position, what his requirements are for a starting hand, what hands he raises with, what kind of hands he calls a raise with, his understanding of his opponents, and whether he will lead bet with a drawing hand. These are just a very few of the questions you need to ask of every player. These clues will mean more money to take home. Here is why.

This observation and the educated guesses that you make when out of the action will stand you in good stead when you are in the action. If you know a person does this or that in certain situations, you will make better choices when you confront that person. When you see the same action, you can make an educated guess as to whether the person has the same thing he had before. Or it could be the opposite. Suppose you have the top two pair in Texas Hold 'Em and so you are worried about trips. If you know what your opponent does when he has trips, you will know he doesn't have trips if he doesn't do what he did before. Get the point?

This is analysis, observation and guesses that will translate into more money for you to take home. Getting a good fix on an opponent is like having extra spending money.

50

Don't Be What You See

The standard advice from poker experts is to play loose in a tight game and play tight in a loose game. In my opinion, this is solid advice. This is especially true in moderate- to upper-level limit games.

If you follow this advice, you will avoid a dangerous and costly mistake that many, many poker players commit. That mistake is to duplicate the type of play that they see at their table. If they get into a wild and crazy, raise-on-nothing game, they will join the jammers and lose track of their own game plan. If you are wise and constantly evaluate the type of game you are playing in and make modest adjustments because the game usually changes from hour to hour, you will avoid getting caught up in the momentum of a "fast" game. You will be aware that you are in a loose game and will tighten up accordingly. If the game gets tight, you adjust and play looser. Constant evaluation of the play and players at your table will allow you to control your game plan and emotions.

AN EXCEPTION

When you find a very loose game, with more than half the players playing almost every hand, you should make an exception to the very tight play theory. Please note that I am writing about very loose games.

The action generated by very loose games increases the size of the pot dramatically. Because of the huge pots, some marginal hands that are throwaway hands for a tight player become playable hands in certain late positions and situations. For instance, in Texas Hold 'Em, suited connectors go up in value in reckless games. I will sometimes play hands as low as eight-nine suited in late position if there is no raise in front of me. If I am running fairly good, I will even call a raise with nine-ten suited in late position when I don't think it will be re-raised behind me. My usual philosophy is this: I do not want to invest a lot of money in hands like the middle suited connectors before the flop. The same is true for hands like k♣–j♥ or q♣–t♠. These hands do not play well in a raised-up berserk game.

In Seven Card Stud I will make more loose calls with three cards to a straight or a flush when I have good position and there are five or more players. If I catch my card on fourth street, then I am usually there to the river.

INSIDE STRAIGHTS

What about it? In these raised-up games, should you ever draw to those notorious inside straights? I will sometimes draw to the inside straight if the pot odds and implied odds justify drawing to the nut straight in Texas Hold 'Em. In Seven Card Stud, I will draw at the inside straight if the odds are good and the cards I need are still live. Usually inside straight draws are just throwaway hands when I am playing tight. One of the beauties of catching an inside straight (and winning the pot) is showing off a new table image that will make your fellow players think you are playing looser than they have perceived.

51

Practice Reading The Opponents

Next to playing a medium-strength hand out of position, the next most expensive "sin" is the failure to pay attention to clues opponents give us. Reading the hand, or perhaps it is better stated as "making calculated judgments on the strength of an opponent's hand," is directly related to our bankroll. As we consider this, we also have to consider the deceptive maneuvers that we all practice. Since these deceptive maneuvers are a part of the game, we need to make some kind of estimate how and how often an opponent uses them. (This will also give us insight into our own use or abuse of these maneuvers.) Does a selected opponent try to conceal the strength of his hand 20 percent of the time? 50 percent? 80 percent? Does he do it only with big pairs or with monster hands after the flop? How often does he represent three of a kind when a pair comes on the flop? Does he bet the nut flush draw 60 percent of the time? We all have different *patterns*. And they are the key to our search.

PATTERNS

Getting a fix on an opponent's patterns is an ongoing dynamic search. It continues as long as we play the game. We are looking for two things: his pattern of play and his pattern of deception. (I play with a man who raises with a pair of tens. He does the same for 10-jack suited). We also need to get a fix on those players who will raise on less than premium hands, and it's especially important to discover what position means to them. For instance, will they raise on K-Q offsuit in middle position? How about A-J offsuit?

I remember a hand I played with Ralph. Ralph is a position-conscious player who would not think of raising in an early position without a premium pair. I put a reliability factor of 95 percent on my judgment of his position play. I was next to last and called on a five-six suited. Ralph raised in the big blind. When the play got back to me it was six-handed, so it made sense for me to call the raise, especially since I felt I knew exactly what Ralph had. For him to raise two places to the left of the button (big blind), he either had a pair of aces or kings. It was even unlikely that he had a pair of queens. The flop came 3-4-7 in three different suits.

Naturally Ralph bet and I as well as two others called. On fourth street, he bet again and I raised him and another man who had turned two pair re-raised. Ralph still called, and I, of course, re-raised. Ralph also called the final bet. My point is that because of his previous play, a fellow player and I knew exactly what Ralph had in his hand. That is the kind of pattern information we need to win the most money. It's also the kind of information we need to keep our play from being too readable.

Whatever game we play in, we need to pick up the clues that are given to us. Some players will have a high reliability factor and others will vary their play enough so that you won't get much of a fix on them.

Tells are great to discover, but careful observations of the patterns is even more profitable. Watch carefully for the pattern of play and the pattern of deception.

52

Change The Pace

Many a young baseball pitcher has a blazing fast ball that serves him well in high school and college ball. That smoke ball will get out most of the hitters, especially if he is just a bit wild and the hitters don't dig in because they are afraid of getting hit. The fast ball becomes his stock-in-trade that he goes to when he needs to get someone out.

Later when the young man gets into professional ball, he finds there are a lot of fastball pitchers and the hitters will stand in the box and take their cuts. It no longer is so easy to get the guys out on just his speed. The pitching coach works with him to develop a change-up pitch that has the same delivery as the fast pitch. If the kid can control that change-up, he will find the hitters will not be able to time his good stuff. In other words, the fast ball looks even faster because they must also be alert for the change. Later, he will develop still another pitch, a three-quarter speed pitch that has the same look as the fast and slow pitch. Then he is really a dangerous pitcher and a force to contend with. His fast pitch is still the main go-to pitch, but when he can get the slower ones over the plate, he has matured as a big time player.

Like the basebal pitcher, you too will develop a style that works for you. You will find through research in books, computers and time at the table that a basic technique will evolve. That system will stand you in good stead because that will be your "fastball." That will be the system you will go to when you want to max out your wins.

Now we need to discuss the "change-of-pace" that will help make you a big leaguer. Everyone develops certain habits when playing poker. We all have a certain favorite way of dealing with a particular starting hand, a raise, an aggressive player, or a passive one. It is important to develop these habits. It gives us a base to work from, a base that works for us. Just keep in mind that habits are easy to spot and you are giving away information about your style that can be used against you.

The change of pace or "changing gears" is important to make your fastball look faster. The real objective for all of us is to plant confusion in the minds of our opponents. We want them to be baffled as to what we are doing, to call our good hands and affirm our bluffs by throwing away their hands. We want them to watch us and fear us. We want them to be confused. We want to be able to read other people's habits and be totally unreadable ourselves.

There are problems with developing confusion in people's minds. For instance, when I am dealt the big pairs in low-limit Texas Hold 'Em, I simply cannot slow-play those rascals. I just can't conceive of letting people into the pot cheaply so they can draw out on me. No, sir, if they want to run me down, they are going to have to pay for the privilege. That is one habit that I just cannot shake. So what I do to compensate for that habit is to raise with a wide variety of other hands *sometimes*. I will pop in a raise with low-suited connectors at certain times. I will even raise in early position with a low or medium pocket pair in Seven Stud and a face card showing. I want people to never know when I have that big pair down below and when I am on a draw.

Learn to change speeds, like the baseball pitcher, practice your control until you can sense when to come with the fast pitch and when to come with the change. When you learn that, you will be ferocious.

53

Free Cards Cost Money

Part One of Four

When you have the best of it, make them pay to draw at you. Don't give them free cards! **Ancient Norwegian Proverb:**

The game was $5-$10 Hold 'Em. Sven, the fellow on my right, showed me his hand before he mucked it. As he did so, he said, "I can never win with these." He mucked a pair of queens. A pair of queens! I was shocked. My eyes darted to the four community cards in the middle. The cards were a jack of diamonds, seven of clubs, six of hearts, and two of spades.

In my head, I recapped the hand. Sven was the second player to act (number four player, because we had two blinds). He had not raised before the flop. Jeff, the man on the button, had raised. The flop came j-7-6. Sven checked and called the bet made by Jeff. When the two came on fourth street, Sven again checked and Jeff bet. This is when Sven showed me his hand and mucked it. Sure enough, Jeff won the pot with j-ace of hearts. Sven had thrown away the winner. Given that flop, I couldn't believe Sven hadn't taken the lead and bet the hell out of those queens.

We have all seen examples of timid play like this. Timid play at the Hold 'Em table is deadly to the bankroll. Sven gave the rest of the players lots of free chances to beat him.

What Sven should have done was to raise before the flop to weed out the players with rags who could get lucky and catch a great flop. A raise might even fold out the big blind. Lots of people will call one bet with an ace-x suited (or even off-suited), or some other rag hand. These are the hands you want to fold.

THAT PAIR OF LADIES

A pair of queens is not an easy hand to play, especially if an ace or king comes on the flop. The aggressive player knows that he must clarify the hand quickly. Hence the raise before the flop. (I much prefer to get queens in early positions than on the button or in one of the blinds. If you can raise early, the rag hands should fold, and if they don't, they are paying a big price to hit a flop.)

Sure, there is danger. Somebody could have a pair of sevens or sixes in the hole and trip up. Or Jeff could have had a pair of jacks, kings or aces. In that case, you lose your chips. My theory is that if I think I have the best hand, I am going to bet until I get raised. I don't ever want to check to the other players and let them have a free card that will beat me. Free cards are bad news.

When you have an overpair, you need to act forcefully and quickly. You want to get clarification as to what is out against you. You do that by betting and raising. This is especially true in the betting round after the flop, before the rates go up (in a structured game). Bet that sucker as quickly as you can. There are many, many cards that can beat you on fourth and fifth street. Any ace or king that hits the board will be a threat. If the board pairs, you could be looking at trips. Act fast and firm with an overpair. Giving cheap or free card(s) before or after the flop is terrible play. Any time you think you have the best hand, make those guys pay to draw at you. Timid play is costly.

54

Free Cards Cost Money

Part Two of Four

When you have the best of it, make them pay to draw at you. Don't give them free cards! **Ancient Norwegian Proverb**

Ted started with 3-4-5 offsuit in low-limit High/Low Split, Seven Card Stud (8 or better for low). He caught an eight on fourth street. A man showing a six-ace checked and Ted checked along. Three other players who started with low cards had caught paints. The hand was checked around and everyone got a free card. Ted now caught a six and the ace-six got a jack. This man checked, Ted checked, everyone checked! two free cards!

Timid play does not pay dividends at the poker table. Ted didn't have a great hand, but it was obvious that no one else did, either. He did have a potential sweep hand; if he caught a seven or a deuce, he had a straight. That is a fair hand. A two or an ace would give him a 6-5-4 low. That is a very strong low hand. By checking he was allowing the others to catch up. This is a dangerous practice.

FREE CARDS CAN COST MONEY

A bet on either fourth or fifth street would help him clarify the relative strength of the opponents. A fourth street bet after the A-6 checked would have helped define who had what. In a structured game, the fourth street bet is only half the price of the bets from there on out.

117

A bet on fifth street would also be called for. Ted had the only made low and good drawing possibilities. He was asking to give his money away.

There are many variables in every situation at the poker table. Let's look at this hand as an example. After the fourth street card, Ted had 3-4-5-8 for low and would have to catch two perfect cards to make a straight. Ted was also looking at another player who had an ace-six showing. However, that person checked! That check had to give Ted a clue. Ted should have factored in whatever information he had about this other player. If that player was a super conservative person who would never bet a good four card low draw, Ted would have to use some caution. However, a bet is still appropriate.

OTHER INGREDIENTS

Some super-conservative players will fold unless they improve on fourth street. When that player caught a six, it certainly looked like an improvement. But he might have a six in the hole or a pair of jacks and would fold if Ted made a bet on fourth street. Other super-conservative players will never lead-bet or check-raise, but will call all bets. They came to play poker and, by damn, they will look at all seven cards. If that is the case in this hand, Ted should bet every chance he can in order to get this guy to put more money in the pot.

There is another reason for Ted to bet with that 3-4-5-8. It is only reasonable that he would win only the low side. Ted should now bet just to increase the size of the pot. The other players are either trying for high or have three-card low draws, which gives Ted an advantage, except for that ace-six.

55

Free Cards Cost Money
Part Three of Four (Continued from #54)

Low-limit games are usually games in which people stay to see most of the cards. High/Low Split is certainly no exception. In fact, High/Low generally has more people competing for the pot because they hope to get at least half the pot. If that is true for your particular game, make them "pay to play" whenever you have a good hand. If you have a chance to sweep the whole pot, be very aggressive.

After the fifth street card, it would be apparent that Ted had a clear advantage (see previous chapter). The ace-six was now an ace-six-jack. When Ted did not bet, he was giving the other players a free shot at beating him.

If you have even a moderate quality hand and you sense weakness from an opponent who is showing good cards, bet to see what will happen. People stay and play rags so often it is incredible. So bet at them until you get raised. Giving them a free card is detrimental to your bankroll.

POSITION

Position has a lot to do with betting strategy. Sometimes you are first or second to act and that is a dangerous place to bet. However, it is important to get information before the betting rates go up in a structured game. And remember, if you bet and get raised, don't automatically call the raise. If the raise was made by someone who plays solid poker and is showing good cards, consider throwing your hand away. If the raise was made by a loose player, consider re-raising. Always be flexible and change speeds often. That way few will be able to read you.

BETTING A HAND

Suppose you start with the 2♠–6♠–4♠ and catch the jack of spades on fourth street. You don't have a great hand but it is certainly worth betting. If you should catch a low spade, say a 7♠, 5♠, 3♠, or, the best of all circumstances, the ace of spades, you will be in great position to sweep. Opportunities to sweep are what you are looking for. If you catch a red king on fifth street, slow down a little. Be sure to count the spades that are exposed and those that are folded. If five or six spades have shown up, not including yours, you might want to fold if the betting gets rough.

A problem card for this hand would be a red eight on fifth street. You would have four parts of a bad low and four parts of a jack high flush (which I consider only a moderate draw hand for high). If you are first to act consider one of two choices:

1. My first choice is to bet and plan to fold if you get raised by a strong player. The person who raises you is putting you on exactly what you have, a poor low draw or spade draw.

2. The other option is to check and face the danger of giving a free card to your opponents. Sometimes you can't avoid giving a free card. As much as you hate to let them get a free one, your hand just isn't strong enough to stand a possible raise. The position and the relative strength of your hand must be weighed. Sometimes poker can be painful. When both choices are bad, I tend to be on the conservative side. Remember the general philosophy: Don't give free cards. They will cost you money.

56

Free Cards Cost Money

Part Four of Four

When you have the best of it, make them pay to draw at you. Don't give them free cards! **Ancient Norwegian Proverb**

The game was 4-8 Omaha. I had 7♣, 8♥, 9♥, 10♠ in my hand on the button. The pot had not been raised, so I called. My heart skipped a beat when the dealer rolled the flop. Two eights and a seven! At that point, I had the nuts. "Check or bet four dollars," called the dealer. Check, check, check, all the way to the man on my right. He bet the four dollars. I was still warm from the flush of victory and simply called the four dollars. After all, I wanted everyone's money, so why raise? Three people called. Do I need to finish this story? You all *know* what happened. A five came on the next card and a queen on the river. I was still counting the chips in the pot as the dealer began pushing them to the guy with the pair of queens in his hand! That no-good had stayed in and drew out on me. A familiar sad story in Omaha. Flop the nuts and get beat on the river. It doesn't feel good.

The only person to blame is myself. I had the opportunity to raise and I slow-played the hand. If I had raised after the four-dollar bet, I'm sure I could have folded the guy with the pair of queens. Except for quads, my advice is never, never slow-play in Omaha. There are too many ways to get beat.

The other day I flopped three kings, filled on fourth, and lost to aces full on the river. This is the way the west is won in Omaha. The guy was drawing dead to one card (I had an ace in my hand) and he hit it. I lost, he won. I didn't feel so badly on that occasion. I had bet that hand as hard as I could. He just paid his money and took his chances with his pair of aces. I want that rascal at my table every time.

A LOW-LIMIT AXIOM

My friend Robert tells me that the fun and profit of low-limit poker is that you get paid off when you have the best hand. That is truth with a capital "T" in Omaha. Your opponents will pay you off with second, third, fourth, fifth nut. So never, never slow play when you have the best hand (quads and unbeatable straight flushes exempted, of course). They will pay you off, so bet, raise, re-raise.

Free or cheap cards cost money. I love it when I get a free card and a free shot at a miracle catch. I would never pay for the chance, but for free, take. The moral is, don't let others get a free shot at you. When you flop or turn the best hand, bet that sucker as hard as you can. Omaha is a game that is won with big hands. When you get that big hand, don't slow-play. If you get beat on the end, then so be it. The French have a saying that applies: "C'est la vie" (such is life). If you get beat, you get beat, but make them pay to draw at their long shots. You will make the most money in the long haul. Low-limit Omaha is a fast-action game. When you have the best of it, play it fast.

57

Don't Mess With The Poker Gods

The poker god was angry! It was 7:00 a.m. when Loren peaked at his cards in the $5-$10 Hold 'Em game. He shuddered. He saw the A-K of spades. "Oh, damn," he said to himself, "How much is this going to cost me?"

"Why," you ask, "would anyone be afraid of the A-K of spades?" For Loren, that previous night was a nightmare. Dozens of times he had started with great cards, like the A-K of spades, picked up a draw or top pair on the flop and got smashed on the last card. Each beautiful hand had extracted a bunch of chips from his stack. Again and again he bought more chips, hoping to turn this trend around. "This can't continue," he kept saying. But it did continue. He lost over two thousand that night.

The deities that control the flow of cards at a poker game take perverse pleasure in giving us a bitter dose of humility. Big or small, gifted or retarded, rich or poor, we all get a long string of good cards that just don't hold up. It is truly horrible. You can change seats, ask for a new deck, walk around your chair, pray — nothing changes the flow. The poker god is ticked off. That is the only rational answer. He (or she) must have a good laugh at us mortals who sweat, fret and swear while desperately trying to keep from going on tilt.

I am *not* referring to short-lived streaks that we get when a few hands get cracked. That is painful enough.

123

For Loren, it was like being put in a torture chamber for twenty hours. It is next to impossible to keep your head together when hour after hour the favorite is defeated by the long shot.

Since the poker god doesn't discriminate, we should be prepared for our turn. Like taxes and death, it will come. If you can't do the best thing, which is to get up and go home, have a contingency plan ready.

FIRST STAGE

The first step is to find your absolute slowest gear. Screw it down as tight as you possibly can, and then take a couple more turns with the wrench. Speeding is strictly forbidden, because the cops are using radar and handing out tickets. Super-low gear is best, crawl up that mountain!

Play only the best of the premium hands. Throw away *all* medium and marginal starting hands. Watch position very closely. Try to keep the action out in front of you. You have an advantage if you are the last to act. Be prepared to wait and wait. The ability to be a leather ass is crucial when coping with an angry poker god.

SECOND STAGE

Once you decide to play a hand, be very careful. As the next cards are dealt or the flops are turned, be anxious to get out. Look for reasons to **not** play, not for reasons to play. That goes against the grain of us action people, but these are not normal times.

THIRD STAGE

Set some goals for yourself:

1. Set a limit for your losses.

2. If you should win a couple of pots and get close to even, cash out. Don't fall into the trap of giving it back.

3. Don't get too tired. When you begin to lose concentration, go home. It is a bitter dose to lose, but your losses can be even worse when you get exhausted.

58

A Basic Mistake

It happened again last night. Frank had taken the empty seat on my right. I was wishing a player of less ability would have sat down because Frank is one tough player. What happened was unusual in this low-limit ($4-$8) Texas Hold 'Em game. Almost always someone will call with some rag hand, but on this occasion, no one called the blind bet. Everyone, including the button, folded their hands!

Frank had the small blind of $2. I had the $4 blind. When Frank called, I jerked in surprise. Frank knows better.

You might ask, "What is wrong with calling one half a bet when heads-up?" A lot is wrong. Let me give you an old Nelson axiom. "Don't run red lights and don't put more money in the pot (limit games, now) when the other person has position on you." Almost always throw your hand away. Get rid of that piece of cheese before it milks more money out of you.

If you call someone who will act after you, there are two distinct disadvantages for you. They are:

1. You *have* to improve on the flop (unless you have a big pair in the pocket). If you check, you can wager the farm that he will bet, and you can't call! You have just thrown away a half bet for no good reason. Give the money to charity and get a tax deduction!

Think about this just a bit. Even if you flop the nut flush draw, you do not have a calling hand. The odds are better than 2-1 against you drawing that flush and you are getting only 1-1 on your money. Remember all you can win in a limit game is one bet, possibly two - if you can check raise. That is extremely unlikely since he will worry about the three suited cards on the board. There just is not enough top side winning potential to justify the risk. So again, listen to the Nelson axiom, dump the hand before it milks you.

2. The second disadvantage is that return on investment I just referred to. Take the actual hand that Frank chose to play. Before he called, there was $6 to contend for. He added $2. He should have known that I would raise with even one face card. I raised with Q♠-8♦. Now there is $12 to contend for. Big deal! Of course my raise challenged him and he re-raised. He ended up losing $42 on the Q♣-7♥ when the board came with an eight. That hand cost him forty-two dollars because his ego got in the way of his normally good sense.

Frank should have let me win the $2 and get on to the next hand when he would have the best position at the table. Pride is a fearful thing.

The same situation applies when you have the big blind, someone raises, and everyone else folds. Unless you have very, very high cards, *get out*! Again, you *have* to improve on the flop or you are dead. There just is not enough money in the pot to justify a battle. Let the other guys win the little battles, you win the war! This game of poker is not about the number of pots we win but about the amount of money we take home! Many, many people see a raise as a challenge to their playing ability. Don't let that happen to you. Play only when the odds are in your favor. Here are two tips. "Don't run red lights and don't put more money in the pot when the other guy has a better position."

59

Look For The Trifecta

I don't bet much on dogs and horses anymore, but I did learn a few of the words. One word has a special application to most games of poker, especially the hold 'em family of games. That word is "trifecta." In our rush to play as many hands as we can, we often forget to be as selective as we should be with our starting hands. When we first peek at our hand, we try to determine if it is good enough to play. Oftentimes we bend the rules so that we can take a chance on a marginal hand. Sometimes this is not a bad thing, as long as we don't do it too often. In the long run, bending the rules on starting hands and playing marginal hands is a losing proposition. What we should keep in mind is what I call the "Trifecta" of hold 'em poker.

My suggestion is that we constantly look for the three parts of the triad: quality of hand, quality of position and quality of the flop. When we can put those three parts together, we have a strong chance of winning.

Whatever hold 'em game you play, Texas Hold 'Em, Omaha Hold 'Em or Pineapple Hold 'Em, be very careful to select only the best starting hands. This is a paramount truth when we are in early position. We just can't play that q♦–j♡♥ when we are the first to act. If you do play it and one or more players raise behind you, you have a real problem! Even if a queen or jack comes on the flop and you have the top pair, you can lose a *bunch* of checks. You have to assume that if the player who raises is a good player, he or she is in there with a premium hand. Now you can play that q-j in late position, if it hasn't been raised. In fact, you should raise with it yourself, especially if you are last. The hand did not change, but the strength added by your position has increased the value of that q-j.

If you are in a tough game of good players, you should not call with small pairs either unless you are reasonably sure that four or more other players will come into the hand. The correct odds to draw to a small pair require about five participants in the hand.

The concept of position is often overlooked by novice and experienced players alike. Good position and the value of a starting hand are closely integrated. As I mentioned, the q-j is a rag hand early, but it becomes a raising hand in late position. That is only one aspect of good position. If you are late or last in the betting round, it is often possible to pick up a pot just by betting at it. You often don't need a hand at all. Also you can get better value for your marginal hands when you are in late position. Suppose you flop the second pair (in Texas Hold 'Em) and it is checked around to you. You can and should bet! It would appear that no one has the top pair and you might be able to win with a marginal hand. If you were in early position, you could not even call a bet.

This third part of the trifecta is the final leg in the process. Start with a good hand in good position. If you should miss the flop, get rid of the hand if there is serious betting. What you want to go with the first two parts is an excellent flop. Then you can make some money and have some fun. If you get just a part of the flop, be very careful. Don't invest much money unless you have the best draw.

60

Calling A Raise With A Marginal Hand

Those readers who have purchased my books in the past know that I write only about low-limit play. Low-limit play has unique characteristics. Low-limit poker also has many, many more participants than high-limit and no-limit poker.

One of the unique characteristics of low-limit poker is the tendency of the players to call a raise with poor- to medium-strength hands. Sometimes it seems to me that these players have no understanding of the significance of a raise. They appear to totally disregard the message sent by the raiser.

"What is the message?" you ask. The usual message is, "I have a better-than-average hand so I am putting you on notice. Call at your own risk."

CALL A RAISE WITH A GOOD HAND

In the low-limit game I play in, this message is often completely ignored. Again and again I see people call that raise cold with not even a decent draw hand! For instance, I raised with pocket queens in a $3-$6 game of Texas Hold 'Em and got called by one guy with k♦-5♠ and another with j♣-7♦. The flop happened to come 5♣-7♥-10♠. That is a great flop for my queens, so I bet

129

and got called by four players, including the two who called my raise cold.

In a wild and crazy game like this one, it is next to impossible to know what the opposition players have in their hands. With that kind of flop I would normally expect at least one caller to have a ten and probably one or more are drawing at an inside straight. I would also guess that someone would have a couple of overcards.

The two "star" players that called me before the flop raise had each flopped a pair. As you can guess, it would take a nuclear accident to get them out of the pot.

The next card was the 3♣. Nothing terribly threatening there except from a possible 4-6. I bet again and got called by the two "stars."

The last card was the j♠. Now I suspect that somebody might have made his hand. I check (not wanting to call a raise) and the j-7 bets. I call. The k-5 calls! The two pair hand had out drawn my queens.

ANYBODY CAN GET LUCKY

So, am I saying that the j-7 made a good play? No way! He made a terrible call of my pre-flop raise! He had to be incredibly lucky to win, but in this case Lady Luck smiled on him.

I want to give Lady Luck an even break. When I start with the best hand, I will win more than the "stars" who rag in behind my raise. I say "God bless" and hope they don't lose their money to someone else.

61

Defending The Blinds In Hold 'Em

Kenny was in the only blind of $3 in a $3-$6 game of Texas Hold 'Em. He held k♠–8♦. Jeff, in number six position, raised and two people called his raise. If Kenny called, it appeared there would be five people in the pot. Jeff was a good solid player. So was Ted, who was in number seven position, and had called the raise cold. In your opinion, what should Kenny do? Should he defend his blind of $3 or give it up?

It is my observation that most low-limit players will defend with almost any two cards. If you are one of those players, this chapter is for you.

If Kenny decides to play that k-8, what could he hope to hit? A king? If a king should flop, he couldn't bet because of his kicker. He has to put both Jeff and Ted on good hands. One or both may have a king and, if so, that king would certainly be with a better kicker than the eight! What about catching an eight on the flop? That might be better, especially if the eight is the highest card on the flop. At least you have a pretty decent kicker and one would not expect someone to be there with an 8-A in this hand. It does happen, of course, especially in low-limit poker. The problem with pairing your eight, even with your king kicker, is twofold:

1. You have no way of knowing if someone has an overpair. Even a pair of nines has you dead in the water.

2. The second problem is the danger of overcards coming on the turn and river. Even if you bet after the flop, you are

not going to drive out the overcards. Not in low-limit. It has been suggested that the check-raise would be a good play in this situation. It might be. If you checked, expecting Jeff to bet as he probably would, then you raised, you might drive out one of the players. If Ted had called the bet that Jeff made, he would probably call your raise and stay to see the turn card. Then if you catch a blank card on the turn, say a 3♦, you might have a chance at the pot. However, any overcard (except a king), of which there are over twenty, would prevent you from betting.

THE REAL PROBLEM

The real problem with defending the blind with a marginal hand is *position*. You just cannot make money on marginal hands from those front positions! That k-8 is a good example. Unless you hit a real long shot flop, say two eights or a king-eight, you have to invest way too much money to see the hand down. You are placing in jeopardy too much money to justify holding on to that k-8.

Now, a draw hand is different. If that k-8 were suited, I would defend my blind, unless there were a big danger that it would be re-raised. With k-8 suited, I can take the flop and be done with it unless I hit a big flop or a flush draw.

A DRAW HAND HAS POTENTIAL

A draw hand is different! If there are three or more players, I will defend a blind as weak as 8-10 suited, 5-6 suited, q-7 suited, q-j unsuited and j-10 unsuited. I will also call with the small pairs when there are three or more players.

General Poker Philosophy To Help You Win

This section of my book is eclectic. Some of these chapters could maybe fit under planning or strategy, but they seemed to me to be better suited to be in this "General" category. This is especially true since I have designed the book to be read a few chapters at a time, not at one sitting.

One important goal I have is to communicate winning designs. I want you to have success at the table, success being defined as having a winning year playing poker. Therefore I next discuss poker prosperity. I also write about using positive reinforcement to enhance your play. I encourage you to have the heart of a lion and be friendly as a lamb. I write just a bit about gambling addiction and being courteous when at the table. I ask the question, "Do you have a tell?" There are many ideas planted in the forthcoming pages. Enjoy and find the gems that will bring you good times.

63

Three "P's" Of Poker Prosperity
(Part One)

I, like any serious poker player, am interested in the profit column. If that column doesn't show a positive balance, something is very wrong. If I lose money in any given week, I have to be concerned. If, God forbid, I lose money for any given month, I must do some serious soul searching! I have to ask, "What is going on? What is wrong with my game that I can change to improve this profit picture?"

Let's take a brief look at three factors that are big contributors to profit or the lack of thereof: patience, planning and position.

PATIENCE

Nothing, in my opinion, destroys the profit potential as much as the lack of patience. When we enter too many pots with marginal hands, when we stay too long when all the signs tell us we are beat, when we draw to long-shot hands, these are all signs that we do not have the patience to wait for favorable circumstances. We try to force a hand when the evidence tells us that we have a slim chance of holding the winner.

It is playing marginal hands in risky situations that causes the problem. The urge to play, to compete for the money in the pot is the culprit. We want to play. We want to compete. That is why we play the game, right? It is like the male vulture says to the female vulture after two hours of waiting: "Patience, hell. I'm going out and kill something!" That is precisely the problem. We get impatient to kill the pot! We want action. We want to risk. We want to play the game.

Unfortunately, to win we must have a bulldog tenacity to wait for the right moment, for the right hand. We must be relentless in our pursuit of that skill to wait, wait, wait. We must develop the conviction to not throw our money into a pot that we are not the favorite to win. We must have the singleness of purpose to dedicate ourselves to winning, not playing. I constantly remind my students I do not teach recreational poker, I teach winning poker. A winning poker player is a patient poker player.

PLANNING

Do you know how to play your big pair after a raise has been made? Are you *absolutely* sure what is the best way? If not, you need to develop a plan.

Do you know for certain how to play a second or third nut full house in High/Low Omaha? Can you fold it if you become convinced you are beat? Do you habitually pay off with a second or third best hand? If so, you need a plan.

Do you call a raise with a small pair in Seven Card Stud? If so, you need a plan.

Do you know when it is time to quit a game because the game is too tough? Do you know how to cope with a bad beat? Do you know how to pick the best game for you to play in? Do you know how to change your play when the mood of the game changes? Do you know how to cope with a losing streak? If you cannot answer yes, you need a plan.

64

Three "P's" Of Poker Prosperity
(Part Two)

I am writing about three *very* important dimensions of your overall poker strategy. The three all begin with the letter "P." Patience, Planning and Position. Let me continue with where I left off in the last chapter, on planning.

General Cromwell said, "Put your trust in God, my boys, and keep your powder dry." Mohammed said, "Trust in God, but tie your camel." How do those sayings apply to poker you may wonder. They say to put your trust in the odds, but also be make provisions for all the bad things that can happen. Have a scheme ready and waiting to throw into the battle should something unusual happen.

I also suggest that you have a master plan to refer to if the need arises, a set of guidelines that you can act on at a second's notice. In other words, have your powder dry, your camel tied.

POSITION

The correct use of position is another vital factor in the profit picture. You will note that quite often in a hand of poker, no one has much of a hand. When circumstances put you in the last or near the last to act, you can often take advantage of this situation and win the pot with a bet.

THE ADVANTAGE OF GOOD POSITION

Whenever you are the last to act, you have a huge advantage over everyone else. They have acted or not acted on their hands without the benefit of knowing what you will do. They are clearly in greater jeopardy than you are. If they have nothing and you have nothing, you have a clear advantage. If you bet, they cannot call you. If they should bet on nothing, they are taking the chance that you have nothing. Sometimes they will be betting into a huge hand and you will raise them and take their money. If they should bet into you when you have a modest hand, they will still be risking a raise because they just do not have the same information you do.

The use of power betting when you have position places a great burden on the people with low-quality hands. They will be intimidated when you bet unless they are laying in the grass, waiting to check-raise. You will soon identify who has the ability to get you to bet their hands and you can accommodate to that as well. The correct play of position is to totally confuse the other players as to what you are doing. Slow-play a big hand once in while when you have the positional advantage. Get their respect. Make them fear you.

65

Have The Heart Of A Lion

Who hasn't seen the gruff man who sits down at the poker table and tries to buffalo the table? He speaks in a loud and commanding manner, he raises with marginal hands and offends the dealers and waitresses. He often comes across as a big buffoon, a blowhard.

However, on the other side of the chip, we have all noticed the quiet, soft-spoken person who somehow commanded the respect of the whole table. When he enters the pot, or, God forbid, raises, a shudder runs through the better players. If the flop comes with big cards, get ready to muck your hand unless you have gotten really lucky. This is a man who demands an accounting. When you next run across one of these quiet, competent players, play close attention to him or her. This person does not play to avoid losing, he or she plays to win. There is a vital and important difference between cautious play to avoid losing and a quiet aggressive player whose every action breeds fear in opponents.

I am reminded of the lion in his native environment. All his actions are slow and easy. He appears more than half asleep, his eyes barely open. The king of beasts is in total command of his situation. When the time is right for action, his movements will be measured and fluid. His actions will be decisive and he will kill what he has chosen to eat. He hunts his game slowly, waiting, waiting for the precise moment to act. That action will be definitive and dynamic. There will be no doubt in anyone's mind what the lion intends to do. The victim has little chance of escape. Supper is served.

THE SHAGGY MANE AT THE POKER TABLE

Ideally, you can be the lion at the poker table. Your appearance will be that of a person half asleep, but the close observer will note that little, if anything, escapes your awareness. When the time comes to enter the pot, your actions are deliberate and smooth. You wait and wait until the moment is exactly right. When you get a situation that precisely correct, there will be no doubt in anyone's mind that you intend to win that pot. The killer, the king of the table, is in contention. He plays to win, not to avoid losing.

Always try to avoid being timid when at the table. Trepidation is not a characteristic that will challenge other players. Play to win. Don't check your good hands. Don't hang back and let the other players take the play away from you. I have seen players call with the absolute nuts, a hand that could not be beaten, and they just call. I keep asking myself, "How can he do that?" He had the winner and yet he did not bet or raise. I understand that sometimes when the cards are running badly and we can't get anything to work in our favor, we can become a bit fainthearted. If that is happening, change tables, quit or take a long break. The good player will breed fear in the hearts of opponents. Like the king of the jungle, play to win.

66

Winning Beats Losing

What does it take to be a winner at the poker table? My grandfather, Nels, God rest his Norwegian soul, told me in clear terms that winning is just one hell of a lot better than losing. Now any old farm boy can sit down at the table and win once in a while. My grandfather was quite clear in saying that it takes a heap of work to become a consistent winner. There is a lot of learning that will have to take place. The question becomes, "Are we willing to pay the price of success?"

What Grandfather Nels was telling me was to "take the game of poker seriously." "Work at it, think about it, develop a game plan." Many people play poker like they drive a car. Once they learn how to drive it, would never occur to them to attempt to improve their skills. That "once learned, always learned" approach to poker is expensive. In poker, the more we know, the more money we make. The more we study and think about the game, the greater our reward.

Another similarity between poker and driving is that there are slow drivers, fast drivers, and the solid drivers who change speeds because the conditions warrant it. They slow down when the roads or traffic are tricky. They speed along when they have clear vision on good roads. The same is true for poker players. There are slow, patient players. There are speeders who love the thrill and danger of playing. There are solid players who can change speed (or gears) as conditions change.

One of my goals in writing the books I write and the teaching I do is to help people develop the ability to recognize what is going on, and adapt (change gears) to the situation. For instance, George had played poker for forty years when he took my class. He had a tremendous fast gear. At the end of the term he thanked me for teaching him the slow conservative gear to use when the cards are running bad. His comment was, "I have lost money for forty years playing poker. Now I am confident I can slow down and protect my winning streaks."

TWO LEVELS OF LESSONS

Poker can be described as consisting of two things: the basics and the nuances (the subtleties). The basics of poker (hand selection, position and preliminary play) can be learned from books. The nuances (clever plays, reading opponents, betting philosophy) generally can be learned only by observant play and thinking about the game. Only a few nuances can be learned from books and classes. Most of the knowledge comes from hours at the table.

I have come to agree completely with my grandfather. Winning does beat losing. I have a *lot* more fun when I am ahead than when I am stuck. So, invest a few bucks in good books, take a class if you can. Learn the basics of which hands to play and the power of position. Most important, think about the game. Study your opponents and yourself. Develop a game play, a betting strategy, and work on the nuances of the game. You will have more fun and have more money in your pocket.

67

Positive Reinforcement

I have a theory to suggest. Why don't you test it out and see if it works for you? I use the reward theory for positive results at the poker table. Simply put, this is it: When I win, I buy something for myself, my wife or sometimes for both of us.

For instance, when I hit a nice win recently, I bought a jacket I had been looking at for a while. Boy, did that feel good to walk in and put down the cash and know that the money was a product of my skill at the table. Another time I was in California playing in a tournament, and hit the boys up pretty good. I went out and bought my wife a real nice outfit, a suit that she could wear when she taught her economics class. She was wonderfully grateful. Need I say more?

REWARDS

I also have another technique for channeling my winnings and rewarding myself. We live on a five-acre track of land with a great view of the mountains, and I wanted to grow asparagus and Christmas trees. In order to do that, I needed a real good rototiller. I compared brands and priced out various tillers and settled on the most expensive one. Then I assigned myself the goal of earning $2,300 over and above my regular poker bankroll. When I reached my goal, I ordered the tiller. What a joy it was to know I had the best piece of equipment available and paid for it with my skill. Every time I start that machine I say a bit of thanks to the poker gods for helping me get a lot of enjoyment from the asparagus and the trees. By the way, the asparagus and trees are part of my long-range retirement goal. Not only do I enjoy the planting and harvesting, but those puppies will give me long-range retirement income. A real sweet deal.

THE BIG BENEFIT

Up to this point I have not mentioned the best part of this reward system. When you set up something like this for yourself, you build a positive reinforcement plan for the future. When you do something nice for yourself or a loved one out of your winnings, you develop better playing habits. You don't just sit down to play poker, you sit down to *win* at poker. That is one huge difference. You know that great things will happen to you over and above the thrill of winning. You know you will have obvious rewards from your study and persistence. You will be able to see and touch the compensation for the travail you must endure to be a good poker player. Because your rewards will be visible, your desire to duplicate your wins will be that much stronger. So the reward system has worked like a pyramid strategy for me. The more rewards I reap, the more rewards I want. In order to get those rewards, my play must continue to improve. That is the benefit for me. Check it out. You might like it.

68

The Expert Trap

If one is to play poker with any seriousness, one should be aware of some of the traps involved with the game. Most of these traps are quite subtle, and any one of us could be in one or more of them without being aware of it. This first trap is one that only good introspection will reveal.

It is my observation, and I hope it is yours also, is that there are a fantastic number of expert poker players. In fact, most of the players you will play with at the low-limit table will be experts at the game of poker. I can hear you ask, "Can that guy over there that just called a bet and two raises with the ace-six offsuit be an expert?" Yes, he probably is an expert. Don't believe me? Let's ask him!

"Sir, me and my buddy here saw that last play where you called twenty dollars cold with that ace-six. You caught a flop of six-six-king and turned an ace. There was over $250 in that pot and you won it all. Tell us, mister. Are you an expert poker player? Have you studied the books, articles and players for many years and developed such an incredible insight into the game as to know when you are going to catch a miraculous flop? You took down a huge pot with what many would call a trash hand. How do you do that?"

Just as serious as a heart attack, he will probably say something like, "Yes, I believe I am an expert. Why one night I was over a thousand dollars ahead in this very game. I knew those guys that raised that last pot were coming in with those big pairs or big suited cards. So I just figured that I could catch a pair of sixes and beat the hell out of them."

"Gosh, sir, you are just the man we are looking for. Would you be willing to share some of your secrets with us? Like, sir, that night you were ahead that thousand dollars, what did you cash out for?"

"Well, that particular night, I did run into a streak of really bad cards and I ended up giving it all back plus some of my own money."

For some unknown reason, normally sane and conscientious men start to play poker and overnight become experts. Perhaps it is something like the Immaculate Conception, where there was divine intervention into the natural laws of the universe.

My advice is to not fall into this trap! To the best of my knowledge, there is no force or power in this galaxy that will give you the fantastic amount of information needed to become an expert in poker. You have to earn your information the old-fashioned way. Plain and simple hard work. Study, practice and deep thinking.

AN OVERNIGHT JOURNEY

I have often marveled at the transition of novice poker players to expert. Since I write books, many of the "experts" laugh at me. Just the other day I was at the table and the subject of my books came up. This one "expert" snorted and said very sarcastically, "How the hell does he have the gall to write books on poker? I have forgotten more than he will ever know about this game." I am quite used to these kinds of comments by now because I have observed the "expert trap" for some years now. By the way, the sarcastic man is notorious for his losing ways. He is one of the guys you and I would send a taxi so as to bring him to the game.

Don't fall into the trap of becoming an overnight expert.

69

Learn A Lesson With Every Hand
(Part One)

Glenna check-raised me after the turn card. Yes, *Glenna*! She check-raised! The lady that is so nice she feels bad when she wins a pot! Glenna occupied the seat to my right. I had a pair of aces in my hand and had raised before the flop. Glenna had already put her $3 into the pot in this $3-$6 Texas Hold 'Em game. She called my raise, along with five other people. Having seven participants in this low-limit game was not uncommon, even in a raised pot. I sent myself a message that I would abandon those aces at the first sign of trouble. Six callers make even that top pair a dog. That is one of the first lessons we should learn about low-limit Hold 'Em.

The flop came k♥–t♥–3♠. No immediate danger in that flop, I thought. The biggest danger would be someone with a k-t. People in the game I play in will call a raise with a k-t offsuit. Don't ask me why, I just rejoice.

The hand I wanted to find out there would be something like an ace-king or king-queen. That would give someone a top pair with a good kicker. He or she would be certain to call all the way to the end.

It was checked around to me, so I bet. Everyone called. Not at all unusual, either. Most consider the $3 a cheap investment to draw for a draw. Say someone had

147

the q♥–6♣. Some will draw for a chance at a heart flush. That is a real long-shot draw, but they could defend it as also having a two-card straight draw. If they should be so lucky as to catch a j♣, they might even raise! I love it.

The next card off was the 3♣. Now I thought that maybe I was in pretty good shape. That gave me two pair and put away anyone playing the k-t. My big danger now was a nine on the river, making someone holding a q-j a straight. Of course, there could always be someone playing a three, but I was willing to take that chance. It is my philosophy that I can't be afraid of every card that hits the board. My feeling is that if I think I have the best hand, I keep betting until someone tells me differently. The way they tell me is usually with a raise. When someone raises, I have to assume they have at least top pair with a decent kicker or else two pair or better.

Again it was checked to me and I bet. Three people called my bet and Glenna check-raised me! I didn't even pause. I just threw my hand away. To my knowledge, Glenna had never in her life check-raised! She is a charming woman who laughs a lot and truly enjoys her poker. However, the best part of poker for her is the social interchange that goes on. She just loves to visit and chat. Without a doubt, she had a full house, most likely three tens and two threes.

My point is that we can learn something every hand. From this particular hand I learned that one player was terribly easy to read had suddenly changed her style. No longer could you tell with high reliability what she had in her hand by the way she bet or didn't bet. The old Glenna would have led bet that set of tens and giggled. Now she was thinking of strategic maneuvers to increase the size of the pot when she had a winner. She was pretty sure that I would bet the pot (which I did), get several callers and then she could come in behind me and collect an extra bet from everyone.

70

Learn A Lesson With Every Hand (Part Two)

This hand with Glenna illustrates that we can learn something from every hand we play. When we stay alert, when we watch patterns and habits, we can indeed learn something every hand. Some good players keep a written log or journal of what regular and/or dominant players do in certain situations. That way they can refresh themselves about how a certain person plays. They can also note when one of them, like Glenna, makes a change and does something different.

ANOTHER ILLUSTRATION

Larry has been a steady player for years. Whenever Larry was in the pot, the better players took note. If he called a bet after the flop, they all made a guess as to what he had. Did he have top pair? Was he on some kind of draw hand? If so, which one? When Larry raised on the last betting round, you had better have a very strong hand or plan to abandon ship. He was the kind of player that you could depend on. When he raised before the flop, you know he had big cards, especially from early position. It was a lead pipe cinch that if he re-raised before the flop, he had one of the big pairs. One day he caught the 7♦–8♦ in early position and raised! He caught a good flop and won the hand. When he showed his cards, the other players almost fainted! The old Larry would never have raised with that hand, certainly never from early position. Who was this new player? Suddenly, everyone had to re-program and change their evaluation of Larry. He had taught them a lesson. That is the kind of thing you should make note of.

As you get more knowledgeable, you will see that players will play differently on different days. While some basic traits will remain, they will play tighter or looser depending on some unknown factor. You have to place these players in the unreliable column and watch very closely for some less-defined patterns.

AN IDEA

Be especially watchful for tricks that you can use to improve your game. Watch the better players. Watch how they manage their money, when they cash out winners, when they quit and why, how they react when on a bad run of cards. Watch how they play the blinds, when they check-raise, when they slow-play, what cards they play from all positions. Poker is a very complicated game and should be approached from the point of view that no one ever learns it all. There is a lesson or two (or even more) to be learned from each and every hand. Keep your eyes open and your mind working. It will pay you rich dividends!

71

The Problem Of Marginal Hands

I have met very few highly disciplined poker players. I have met no perfect poker players. I have met lots of poor players and lots of marginal players. It seems to me that most of us who love this game play too many hands. That includes the poor players, the marginal, the better, the intermediate, and the advanced players. We play too much. So you ask, "Isn't that what poker is all about? Who wants to sit and watch others compete for that pot?"

Oh, yes, that is indeed the problem! When we throw away a hand that we might have played, and then it turns out that we would have won, we are frustrated. "Why didn't I take a chance and play that pair of fours (in Seven Card Stud)?" We moan to ourselves (and others) that that pot was really ours and vow to never fold a winner again. Or we fold a 9♣–4♦ in late position of Hold 'Em and the flop comes 4♣–4♥–9♠. We don't realize that the flop was a miracle flop and you could play that 9-4 until doomsday and not catch that one again. Or that somebody with a pair of jacks in their hand catches a jack on fourth street for jacks full of fours and we would have won a big bunch of our money.

Playing marginal hands is a huge temptation in poker. We all love to play and it is a constant battle with ourselves to not play trash.

The big problem with playing a marginal hand is not in the initial bet that we call. Sure, that depletes our stack, but the danger is *after* the next card or the flop. Just suppose we play that pair of fours when a king has raised. Then we catch a card that gives us three to a flush and three to a straight. So now we have several outs and rationalize that we can get lucky and beat that pair of kings. So we call another bet! *That* is the problem I am talking about.

In Texas Hold 'Em, suppose we play a 5-6 offsuit in early position. The button raises it and so we call another bet. Then the flop comes 4-8-9 with four players taking the flop. Now we have a real trap hand. So we call another bet and the turn card is a six. Now what? We have at least three betting units invested. Do we fold? We still have that inside straight draw and a pair to go with it. By now it is heads up with the raiser. We think "Well, maybe he raised with k-q or a-j." Of course, but he could have raised with 10-10 or 9-9 also.

Do you see what I am driving at? When we weaken and do play a marginal or trash hand, we often get trapped into putting more money in the pot on a long shot draw. That is dumb.

My advice is that if you do enter a pot with a marginal hand (I won't even comment on a trash hand!), do so with the knowledge that you do indeed have a poor chance to win, and unless you get very lucky on the next card or the flop, you will be done with the hand. If you are aware that you are on thin ice and if you can tell yourself that you will only continue to play if you get a great hand or a high-percentage draw, you have a much better chance of ending the session with a win.

Now I am not saying you should never take a shot at winning on a marginal hand! There are times and places where it is appropriate to do so. Say you have an A-3 on the button in Texas Hold 'Em and nine people call with no raises. Certainly go ahead and play. The odds are close enough for you to call. If you hit your hand, terrific. If you miss, throw it away. But don't get suckered into calling another bet unless you have a good chance.

72

The Importance Of Marginal Hands

Marginal hands are a curse! Marginal hands are like pretty women in scanty costumes, standing on street corners, they have no last names, and they suck your money away. They promise you much and deliver little. They look great, but lack substance. They are seductive and cute, yet they devour your bankroll. Now you are warned! You play with them at your own risk.

Marginal hands AND women with no last names can offer some entertainment, if you understand them and know how to control them. There is one major difference. The girls will cost you. Careful play on marginal hands *can* make you some money.

THEY ARE LEGION

In any poker game, the number of marginal hands is only exceeded by the number of trash hands. I categorize hands into only three groupings: premium, marginal and junk. Junk hands are no problem, and quite often premium hands play themselves. It is the damn marginal hands that cause the problems. However, it is those same damn hands that offer monetary remuneration if we can learn to play them to our advantage. It ain't easy, but those marginal hands can be a source of profit for us. A word of caution: These hands have to be played very carefully. Again, those hands are legion. With skill and caution, those hands can show a profit for us.

SKILL AND CAUTION

The absolute key to playing a marginal hand is position. Since it is taboo to call a raise with a marginal hand, you must be almost positive that there will be a minimal charge to enter the pot. Why is it taboo to call a raise with a marginal hand? Just ask yourself the question, "Why enter a risk situation where you are not the favorite?" That is real money you are putting on the line. It is better to give the money to your church or charity and get a receipt that is tax deductible than to waste it on a marginal hand. A marginal hand, by definition, is a draw hand. You must improve it to win in most situations. If you have a huge draw hand, that is not a marginal hand. A huge draw hand might even be the favorite. That is when you put in a raise. So position is the fundamental principle in calling with a marginal hand.

A marginal hand in a Seven Card Stud game would be J♥–4♥–8♥. That hand has marginal value, especially if more than two other hearts are exposed. The hand's value is further reduced if either the ace of hearts or king of hearts is exposed. These exposed cards decrease your chances of improving to a flush or a better flush. (You have observed that quite often when one person has a flush, one or more flushes are also present.) If you are in a very late position, you can call with that hand. If you catch a heart on fourth street, especially a big heart, you now have a good hand.

CAUTION AND AGGRESSION

Now is the time for a combination of pugnacity and caution, a strange combination. You want to bet your hand and get paid off when you make it, however, you must be aware that someone can beat your flush. Be very, very alert to a higher flush possibility and for someone to catch a full house.

73

A Lesson To Be Learned

In the course of years, I have had several professions, or ways of earning my living. I grew up on a farm in Minnesota and have worked as a carpenter, lumberjack, and banker, among other things. In all of those jobs, there are certain "tools of the trade," one has to learn to be successful. As a farmer, my father taught me how to repair machinery and engines. He constantly preached maintenance as the key to getting the crops planted and harvested. One had to listen and watch for any weakness or problem in the machine. If you were alert, you could often prevent a major breakdown that would cost you valuable time and money.

As a lumberjack, I certainly was aware that my Stihl chainsaw had to have hourly maintenance. The oil and gas had to be added regularly and the chain sharpened in a timely fashion. If I were to have production, I had to take care of my tools.

As a carpenter, careful use of tools was also critical. Even as a banker, my tools were knowledge of people and knowledge of regulations and rules.

Whatever the job or profession, one must know what tools are needed and how to maintain them if he or she is to be successful. There are lots of sloppy carpenters, farmers, lumberjacks, bankers, etc., who do not use their tools very well. It is the person who takes his work seriously who rises to the top. That person is constantly studying, working, maintaining. That person knows that his or her paycheck is dependent on how much information he or she has and how well the tools of the trade are maintained.

The "tools" of a successful career in poker are not chips and cards. They are knowledge, betting courage, patience and emotional control. Your year-end-profit will be determined by how well you know and maintain those tools.

Knowledge of odds and probabilities can come from books and discussions with experienced players. This knowledge is a primer for any kind of serious poker. You also just plain have to comprehend a certain set of numbers before you can become a winning player.

When you know that "certain set of numbers," you will recognize advantageous situations when you are the favorite to pull down the pot. When you find that favorable circumstance, you must have the courage to bet and raise it up. That is easy to do when the cards are running your way. However, when you are in a bad streak and you are catching poorly, it takes real courage to lay out that extra money.

Patience is an incredibly important tool. As I tell my students, poker is about 50 percent skill and 50 percent patience. If you don't have the skill, you damn well better have the patience.

How many times have you seen someone absorb a bad or tough beat and just go absolutely ballistic? They rant and rave, throw money at the pot in an attempt to get back the money they lost. A small percentage of the time they will succeed, buat most of the time they lose big time. You simply cannot power poor cards into winners, especially when on tilt. The good players will recognize your emotional state and simply call you down. They will make you prove you have the best hand. Emotional control is an absolute must for you to develop. It is one of several tools that must be honed and worked on constantly.

74

Pace Your Playing

Poker is truly an attractive game. But poker is also addictive. It is quite common for a player to sit down and play poker all night. As the sunlight gradually peeps through the blinds, most players are bleary eyed and some are even asleep as they wait for the next deal. The attention level is distorted by fatigue. Many mistakes are made at this time because the optimal awareness has long since gone away. When this happens, you are at a disadvantage unless you have conditioned yourself to marathon play.

DO NOT BE A DISADVANTAGED POKER PLAYER

When you play poker, play to win. One of my favorite themes is, "Winning beats losing." So play to win. Playing to win means to always try to position yourself to play with the best possible chance to beat whatever game you are in. If you play with the same bunch of guys every week or so in someone's home, you are probably not disadvantaged by the physical setting or being unfamiliar with the players.

It is quite a different story if you go somewhere and play in an unfamiliar game. This happens when you go to Vegas, California, Maryland, or wherever you have not played before. The setting is dramatically different, with different house rules, games and systems. The new setting requires you to expend energy just to adjust, which takes something away from the energy that should be devoted to your attention span and concentration on the game and players.

MAKING THE QUICK READ

On many occasions I have played in the card rooms in Nevada and California. Each and every time I sit down at the table in those settings, the demand to study each and every player is clear. I watch each and every hand that is turned over and mentally back up and replay the hand to get a clue as to how that particular player has responded. Has he called a raise with his starting hand? Has he raised? What was his position? Did he appear to know what other players would likely have? Is he a smart player? Does he start with a marginal hand?

These are just a few of the questions I ask myself as the game progresses. When you don't have a fix of any kind on any of the players, you try to accumulate information ASAP. This quest for knowledge requires energy and concentration that sometimes tap the well of my energy. There is only so much energy available for quality play within an eight-hour stretch. When that energy is expended, I will be at a disadvantage if other players have a better supply of energy. Program this energy drain into your computations regarding how long you should play in a particular game. Do not play beyond your limit. Don't play with and empty tank. It could very well cost you money.

75

Courtesy At The Table

Who among us hasn't heard a diatribe by a self-styled authority on poker aimed at a lesser player who has just put a huge beat on him? You can see the smoke coming out his ears. It is really funny if it were not so sad. This "master" of poker is giving this poor tourist a reading out that reminds me of a mother bear cuffing her cub. He depreciates the poor tourist and ridicules his play. "How could you draw to that hand? What were you hoping to catch? Don't you know the odds against catching your only winning card?" On and on he goes, and all the time this "lesser player" is stacking up the chips, afraid to even look up. He feels embarrassed enough to pick up and cash out, and the "expert" has lost all chance of getting his money back. The tourist goes back to Dubuque and will never play poker in that casino again. "Nice going, big shot!" is what I want to say. "You drove off the best source of new money we had."

I can understand how this "poker authority" felt. I hate like hell to lose to a long-shot draw, but that is the dynamic nature of low-limit poker. One should come to terms with that style of play in low-limit or just not play. Bad or tough beats are as inherent to low-limit poker as hearing loss is to the elderly. It is one of the factors we have to cope with.

While I can make a good case for the wisdom of not disparaging a bad player, the primary reason for not being critical is not financial. *The foremost basis is plain and simple courtesy.* We are human beings sitting down to compete with each other. When I denigrate you, I denigrate myself. I am less of a person when I put you down because we are all a hunk of hair, a bit of flesh and victims of the universe. We are all in this crazy messed-up place together and there is only one way out. Being cruel to one another does not compute.

USE DECEPTION, NOT RIDICULE

In one of the early columns by John Vorhaus in The Card Player, John counsels us to compliment a player who catches his lucky card and beats us out of a pot. In fact, he says, "Charm him. Make him feel warm and fuzzy. Foster within him the illusion that he actually knows how to play." I can agree with John. It is by far the best thing for our financial well-being to help that person continue to make bad plays. If we can compliment him, he will stay longer and maybe reinvest his chips into pots that I can win. Since the game of poker is legitimately about deception, we can do this with a clear conscience. I don't think we are depreciating the person with this kind of ploy. This ruse is perhaps a bit shady, but quite well within the ethics of the game. Anywhere else this kind of deception would not be considered courteous. The game of poker permits, yes, even encourages, deception as long as it is not cheating. Any kind of cheating is beyond the pale, but cunning is admired. As long as we do not devalue the person by criticism, we can fall within the boundaries of courtesy. We must not depreciate this person, but we can cajole him into thinking he is a good fellow for playing with us.

76

What Is Confidence?

How do you get confidence? Is confidence a way of thinking positive? Or is it more than that? Since confidence is an important component of winning, let's take a close look at what it means. First, a dictionary definition of confidence:

confidence: a. faith or belief that one will act in a right, proper, or effective way. b. a feeling or consciousness of one's powers or of reliance on one's circumstances. c. a state of mind or a manner marked by easy coolness and freedom from uncertainty. d. objectivity in assessing one's own power.

Here is what a noted writer, William Pitt, says about confidence:

I cannot give them my confidence; pardon me, gentlemen, confidence is a plant of slow growth in an aged bosom: youth is the season of credulity.

Further, let us search a thesaurus for words that can give us further clues. There we find: assurance, aplomb, poise, self-possession, conviction, determination, surety.

William Pitt suggests that the path to confidence is a long one. Confidence is not achieved quickly: it must be earned. Confidence is the product of talent, training and dedication. Confidence "radiates" from within because it comes from long years of labor. Confidence comes because you know you know. You must have the track record to prove it to yourself. (It isn't so important to prove it to others as it is to prove it to ourselves.) You have power because you know you have power. You have internal coolness because you are cool inside. You have surety of purpose because you are objective in assessing your own power. You have poise because you have earned poise under stress and trial.

Confidence translates into power at the poker table because you are absolutely certain of your ability to beat whatever game you are in. You do not brag about any exploit or a superior knowledge; you simply know you are the best. There is an aura about you that translates into something to be feared. If luck turns against you for a while, you simply wait quietly for luck to turn. You do not whine and complain. You are perfectly at ease with yourself and your expertise. You need to convince no one that you are the best. You are who you are and that is an unshakable conviction. Let the wanna-bes strut, posture and brag. You have no need for such behavior. You could quite simply wear a Sherman button to a Georgia picnic. You wouldn't, of course, but you have enough faith in yourself to do so.

This inner certainty is a powerful force to take to the table. It is not easy to attain and cannot be faked. You must earn it, the old-fashioned way — plain and simple hard work.

It is easy to confuse confidence with arrogance or boldness. Those are surface attributes that do not communicate the burden of conviction. Arrogance is flashy, trite and superficial. Arrogance does not have humility and courtesy as its base.

When you encounter true confidence at the poker table, beware. That person will take home some of your money. To answer my opening question "How do you get confidence?" My answer is just two words: hard work. The only truly valuable things in life have to be earned.

77

Choose Your Opponents Carefully

I am reminded of my fourth-grade teacher. God bless her soul, she turned my young life around because she cared for me. The one thing she would say to me often was, "Andy, pay attention *now*." That was my signal to quit daydreaming. *Now* was the time to quit gazing out the window, to pull my thoughts together to some point of history, math, geography or grammar. My mother was also most grateful to that teacher. What that dear teacher taught me in fourth grade has, believe it or not, carried over to the green oval poker table. There are some very important moments when I must indeed remind myself to pay attention now.

THE EDUCATED PLAYER

Let's talk about what the informed player does while watching a poker game in session, whether he is sitting at the table or waiting to get a seat.

What a good player looks for when watching the game is to identify the general playing styles of each player. Information is gleaned about one or more players on every hand. If any cards are visible, like in Seven Card Stud, an educated player can make a decent guess as to the strength of a hand by the porch and the betting or calling pattern. For instance, if an aggressive player is showing four big cards in one suit and checks it when there is nothing threatening about the other hands showing, you can usually determine that he does not have his flush. (You must be careful that he isn't hoping to check-raise.) Of course there are several other possibilities if a person doesn't bet when he has a good porch. One is that he could be a timid better and is afraid that someone else has a higher flush or hit their two pairs draw to hold a full house. All of these possibilities are clues.

The educated player watching the game is paying attention to all these possibilities. This information is pivotal for profit. The matrix of each and every hand is complex. The good player looks first for the general level of competency of each player and then refines his opinions as he gains more data.

I was playing with a group of players I had never seen before. The game was Texas Hold 'Em and one player raised from early position. When the hand was shown down, he had a pair of twos in his hand. He immediately went into my "flake" category. Later he re-raised with an ace-four offsuit, hit two runners to make a straight with his four. I then moved this player into the "dangerous, but love to have in the game" classification.

> Sidenote: Doesn't low-limit poker have some wonderful characters? And when they win, it is really fun to watch them.

The game of poker has so many subtleties that it can hold a lifetime of fascination to an alert player. Success, though, is centered around being able to do what my teacher advised, "Pay attention, *now*."

78

Money Moves Counterclockwise

Don't we love the donators? Don't we appreciate the guys and gals who sit down and call every hand? Or those who raise with trash?

When we get lucky to have a novice heavy-duty player at our table, we should have some strategies to cope with their table presence.

THE EASY ONE

Clearly the easiest player to develop a coping scheme for is the calling station. He or she is involved in each and every hand. They will seldom raise or re-raise, and, when they do raise, it is a definite read on the strength of their hand. The best coping method for the calling stations is to encourage them to keep on playing. Be friendly. Make them feel welcome. You want these people to play as long as possible.

THE DIFFICULT ONES

Boy, if only the novice, aggressive scary players were so easy to counter and manipulate. Some of these people are very difficult to play with and make it hard for you to show a profit.

One very well-known strategy is to attempt to sit to the left of the aggressive player. The rationale, according to expert poker player/writer, Mike Caro, America's Mad Genius of cards, is that money moves clockwise. Therefore, since this aggressive player is an active participant in the game, you want to be able to choose the times when you compete with him. If you act after he has put his money in the pot, it becomes your option as to whether or not you compete. When you do enter the action, you will come in with good quality hands. When you enter the pot with a top- quality hand, the odds are in your favor. That is exactly the posture you want.

FIXED POSITION GAMES

A special consideration must be made for the fixed position poker game (Texas Hold 'Em, Omaha, etc.). An aggressive player on your right can cause problems when you have the blind(s). When you know that he will raise with marginal or trash hands, you are more tempted to call. Seeing him raise and drive you off the pot you would have won causes frustrations. These frustrations are important because they can cause you to lose some money.

DON'T FORGET THE OTHER PLAYERS

One very important cosideration to keep in mind is that we tend to forget about the other players who are less pushy. The aggressive player commands so much attention that we lose touch with what the other players are doing. This is low-limit poker, and aggressive play will typically not force good hands to be thrown away. Watch carefully that while you beat the clown, you do not lose the pot to another player.

One very important advantage to having either type of contributors in your game is the size of the pots. Some of them can be huge. So watch and wait.

79

The Best Of Intentions

I remember my mother saying, "The road to hell is paved with good intentions." As a young squirt, I really didn't know what she meant. It was only as a grown-up that I found out that life has lots of pitfalls, one of which is "intending" to do something. I "intended" to earn my first million by the age of thirty. I "intended" to marry a rich and beautiful girl who was without faults. I "intended" to never bend the rules.

When most of us sit down at the poker table, we "intend" to play our best poker. What happens? Right off we catch a pair of fours in late position in a Seven Card Stud game and we are so anxious to get into the action that we call a raise. Or the hole cards are j♦–t♠ in a Texas Hold 'Em game in early position and we call with it and the pot gets raised by the guy on your left and everyone drops out. We call. Bad, bad, bad! The road to hell — and poverty is paved with good hand-selection intentions. Our desire to play the game overrides our good judgment.

Alexander Pope wrote, "It is not so much the being exempt from faults as the having overcome them that is an advantage to us." I take that adage to mean it is okay to have some problems, but it is by far better to be able to surmount the obstacles.

When I try to translate that concept into practical poker terms, I come up with a plan to turn around my tendencies to get involved in situations I should not be in, like playing too many marginal hands. Sure, I love to compete for the money. Sure, I love the action. Sure, I want to play catch-up and run down that guy who ran me down last time with a trash hand. Sure, I love to make a big hit and cash out for big money. We all have those tendencies. That is why poker is so attractive and popular. But those are the "faults" that I was born with.

OVERCOMING THE FAULTS

We should not be ashamed of those faults. Those faults come to us because we are human. The lesson we need to learn is that we must change our priorities from wanting to play in too many pots to being more selective. However, it takes more than good "intentions" to succeed at overcoming these weaknesses. We must take very positive resolutions to fight the yearnings of too much action.

Let me illustrate what I do with my poker students. Since we all have this craving to enter, I make the assumption that all the students have that craving. I tell each and every class that the key to profit in poker is in the wrist. In other words, pick those cards up and throw them away. Use the wrist to discard those marginal and poor hands before they cause you to lose money. The way to overcome the fault of playing too much is to flex your wrist. Don't just "intend" to throw borderline hands away, do it. Practice, practice, practice throwing cards away. Your intentions won't save you money — the wrist will save you money. It works. Unless you curb your longing to play, you cannot win in the long run.

Another theme to develop: You don't go to the doctor and throw away the prescription he gives you. So don't read and study and not apply it.

80

Win Big Pots

I see it all the time. And it happens because fairly sophisticated players make a basic mistake. That basic error is another instance in which you let your ego get involved. Take this scenario:

The game is Texas Hold 'Em and the big blind has Q♠–2♠. Everyone folds except the button who raises. The little blind folds and it is your option to call, re-raise or fold. What do you do? You have the strong suspicion the guy is stealing and you dislike him intensely. Again, what do you do?

Do you call and hope to catch three spades? Do you call and hope to hit three deuces? Do you call and hope to hook two pairs?

All of these flops are real long shots. But do you tell yourself that you have to teach that guy a lesson?

Do you see how the ego can get you into trouble?

The real basis for your decision should not be ego, but a bottom-line factor. Ask yourself how much you can win with this situation. Now that is easy math. No problem there. All you can possibly win is whatever he is willing to put in. Then factor in the times you will lose to him, because sometimes he will have a better hand and sometimes he will just plain draw out on you. So the big question is, "Why risk it?" The guy has you hammered on position and can make you pay big time if you catch a fragment of the flop and try to improve. If you don't improve on the flop at all, which is most likely, he will bet and you can't call. Why throw money at a losing proposition or, at best, a very limited win?

The basic mistake is trying to win all the pots. The number of pots is not the primary factor. The *size* of the pots you win or want to win is the main consideration. So don't waste your checkers when you are in an unfavorable situation or going uphill. A huge number of players make this basic blunder.

It is vital that you avoid adverse situations and to amplify favorable positions. There are many times in the course of a poker session that you will have an opportunity to build big pots in which you are the favorite to win. The nut flush is the most common occurrence in Texas Hold 'Em and a moderate or high set in Seven Card Stud. Let's look at the nut flush draw which should be raised if three conditions are met:

A. There are at least three other players

B. You are in late position or can check-raise. If you raise from early or middle position, you are likely to drive out the players you want to call. It is usual in low-limit poker for players to put in the second betting unit if they have already called one betting unit.

C. When the board is not paired. If the board is paired, you should only call when you are in very late position and the pair on board is not a medium or high pair.

Say you are in a Seven Card Stud game and you catch three of a kind. You are a big favorite in most situations. You want to make the flush and straight draws pay dearly. And you have a reasonable chance to beat them even if they hit their draws because you have about a 40 percent chance of improvement with three cards to come, a 33 precent chance to improve with two cards to come and 22 percent chance with one card to come.

81

Reading An Opponent (Part One)

Charlie grunted when the next round of cards was dealt. He wasn't grunting at his own card because he hadn't looked at that yet. He was watching what Rose and The Bandit had caught. The game was Seven Card Stud and Charlie had aces and sevens. Rose was now showing three hearts and The Bandit had paired his door card, a ten. Charlie knew he was in trouble unless he made a full house. His card was the three of clubs. Rose bet and The Bandit called. Charlie cheerfully mucked his hand. Why you ask? Because of *aperçu*. What in the world is aperçu? Believe me, it isn't that I am trying to impress you with a big vocabulary or throw big words around. What is most important to me is to communicate effectively, and the word aperçu has come to mean a lot to me as I play poker. This is especially true when trying to get a read on other players. Here is the definition of aperçu as given by Webster's Ninth Collegiate Dictionary.

Aperçu: 1. An immediate impression; esp. INSIGHT 2. A brief survey or sketch: OUTLINE.

This is what reading people at the poker table is all about. I must get an immediate impression of what my fellow players are holding. I must try to gain an insight into the strength of their hand by the clues I have observed. I must formulate a sketch or outline of how they are playing this hand and make a decision as to whether I should continue to play my own hand.

171

Obviously, if I think they have me beat, I fold. If, on the other hand, I have a well concealed monster hand, I would like them to take the lead and sucker some other people into the pot before I reveal the true strength of my hand. I want them to have a good, second best hand and call me all the way. So if I can do a good job of aperçu, I maximize the money I make on my best hands and minimize my losses on my second best hands.

Developing the ability to read my opponents effectively is a constant, minute by minute struggle. It takes lots and lots of dedicated practice to become proficient at aperçu. Here are a few ideas to help you:

Read the best book around on this subject, *Book Of Tells* by Mike Caro, The Mad Genius. This book is a classic and is regarded as a textbook for some classes in poker playing. It is still available for only about $20 in hardback — a *very* reasonable price for what you get. The illustrations are terrific, Caro's analysis of what is taking place in the photos is great and he also includes a reliability table. This book is a must for serious poker players.

In addition to looking for "tells," develop the habit of logging patterns displayed by certain opponents. Terry will almost never raise with a pair of kings or queens from any position in Texas Hold 'Em. He will raise with a pair of aces, except on the button. Joyce will play a k-5 offsuit, Helen will never check-raise, and Steve plays tight except when he has the best position and then takes some big chances. These are the sort of things you want to remember. I have found it valuable to write these things down. I keep a loose-leaf logbook and have each page dedicated to only one player. Whenever I find a new pattern about a certain person, I write it down.

These are two ideas to help you develop aperçu. It is those lighting-fast conclusions that will increase your earnings from the Friday night game or from your local poker club.

82

Reading An Opponent (Part Two)

As soon as you sit down at a new game, try to get a general fix on each player. The four big categories (for simplistic purposes only) are loose, super loose, average and tough.

1. A loose player will play most of the hands, but the key to identifying him is the quality of hands he displays. When he turns over a very marginal hand from early position or after a raise, he will slide very easily into the loose category. For instance, if he calls a raise when he has two pairs and the board shows three to a flush or something like 7♥–8♦–9♣–t♥ in Texas Hold 'Em, slip that person into the loose category. If he calls a raise from a person with an ace showing in Seven Card Stud and he has a ten showing and another ten folds across the way, watch to see what he turns over. If he drew to a pair of tens after the raise and either did not see the exposed ten or didn't care, this person is definitely a loose player.

Please be aware that these or only a few of hundreds of things a loose player will do. Develop your own list of distinguishing characteristics. In most low-limit games, you will find an abundance of players who will fall into the loose grouping. (I am certainly making the assumption that you are not one of these!)

2. The super loose will play almost every hand. An easy tipoff.

3. The average player will play around 40 to 50 percent of the hands in most low-limit games that I play. They usually have some idea of the value of position and will usually have fair starting hands. They do tend to overplay nonconnecting suited cards as a general rule. They will often call a raise with any two suited cards in a Texas Hold 'Em game and won't watch very carefully what cards are folded in a game of Seven Card Stud. For instance, they might call with three hearts and not know there are four other hearts showing. Or they might have three cards to a low straight and not be aware that most of the cards they need to finish the straight are no longer live in the deck.

4. The tough player is just about as easy to spot as the super loose player. The tip is about the same, except it is the opposite: He plays only a very few hands. He will seldom play a hand from early position, and, when he does, be notified that if he calls after the next card, he probably has a decent hand. Beware. A couple of tips will help you here. If he smooth-calls a raise, he either has the nuts and slow-playing, or he has the nut draw. There are at least two good reasons for slow-playing:

A. To keep others in and get their money.

B. He will check-raise if he feels the situation is appropriate, .

If the tough player does check-raise from early position, you can be assured he has one of the very best hands. That kind of player does not expose that kind of money unless he has a terrific chance to take down the pot.

Another valuable clue as to the strength of his hand is if he cold calls a bet and a raise. If he calls two raises, you can be dead certain he has the nuts or is drawing at the nuts. This kind of a player is fully informed about pot odds and implied odds. He will only put his money in the pot if he feels there is a good return on his money.

83

Concentration

How important is concentration for your win/lose ratio? My guess is that we would agree that concentration is terribly important. However, here is a scenario that might be familiar. On the way to the poker game, I have my little discussion with myself about patience, starting hands, emotional control, etc. When I arrive at the game, there are four or five guys I know and we spend a few moments kidding each other. I tell this one guy that he should take good care of himself because if something happened to him, I would be the ugliest man in the world. You know how this kidding goes. Sometimes this kidding gets out of hand.

BEING FLIPPANT COSTS ME MONEY

I am still in a flippant mood when I sit down behind my chips. We are still talking smart to each other. I crack wise a couple of times and play a marginal hand because I feel lucky. That hand gets cracked after I take it one card too long and I am stuck $27. I think, "What the hell are you doing, Andy?" That glib feeling of being among friends has cost me some money. What did I lose? I lost $27 and my concentration.

When I sit down at the table, I want to be focused. I want to be centered. I want to win. I want to have all my intellectual powers concentrated on the game.

Talking smart and having a good time with the guys is a great feeling and sometimes I get carried away. Life should not be all business and directed, but when money is so dynamically related to concentration, I honestly fault myself for doing something I know is not in my best financial interest.

CONCENTRATION CREATES CONFIDENCE

Perhaps you have noticed how success breeds success in poker. I believe that success is directly related to the confidence you have in yourself. When I can focus — when I can concentrate on the game, read the player's habits and tendencies, carefully watch my own play and hand selection, play after the initial decision to enter the action — my concentration communicates to the other players that I am serious about taking their money. I want the other players to fear me. I can gain that fear by concentrating on the game. When I sense that fear in them, my confidence rises. Unless I get put on tilt, which is happening on only rare occasions nowadays, concentration pays off. I love to talk smart with my friends, but talking smart has cost me bucks. So I try to smart talk away from the table, either over the lunch counter or over the phone. The poker table is clearly the wrong place for me to lose concentration!

84

Speed Thinking

Is fast thinking a gift at birth or can it be developed?

Poker is a game of speed. This is particularly true in a casino or card club setting where there is a center dealer provided by the club. The dealer has an interest in keeping the game moving quickly because he makes most of his money on tips. Therefore, the more hands he gets out, the more money he makes. The better dealers will encourage you to act quickly. They do this in subtle and overt ways. Their subtle ways are by acting quickly themselves, and overtly by pointing to you, speaking your name and suggesting you act.

Most of the time you will not need extra time to decide what you want to do. However, there are times, important times, when you must make a critical decision. Quite often, an extra second or three will help you make the best choice. Here are three suggestions on ways to improve your speed and obtain the extra seconds that you might need:

A. I am a firm believer in looking at your hole cards as soon as they are delivered. If I should catch a marginal hand, I want to check out my position and the quality of the players yet to act. If I should catch a premium hand, I want to be able to ascertain the best way to bet this hand to maximize the potential profit. One trick I use in Seven Card Stud is to try to sit in number one or two seat to the left of the dealer.

That way I get my cards a few seconds before the other players and I can plan some strategy.

B. If I need some extra time and the dealer is looking at me, expecting me to act, I will often hold up one finger. This is the non-verbal way of telling the dealer, "I'm with the hand, but I need to consider my options. Please wait just a bit." Another way is to verbally ask for time. This communicates the same message.

C. By far the most profitable way to speed up your reaction time is to do a good bit of homework. Take the time to mentally work through what you believe to be the best way to react to any one of several common situations. For instance, have a plan in mind for when you catch the big pairs, what to do with rolled-up trips in Seven Card Stud, when to raise to obtain a free card, and when to semi-bluff. If you have baseline reactions to these usually profitable situations, your reaction time will often be shorter and you will most likely have a more profitable session. The more of these relatively common situations you are prepared for, the more accurate your betting will be.

BETTER OBSERVATIONS

There is another direct benefit from speed thinking. If you have prepared in advance, you will be much more observant of the other players and be able to pick up clues from them. If you are focused only on your hand and how to play it, you won't be as observant of others as you could be.

Most of us are not terribly gifted with speed thinking. Therefore we need to find and use the tricks to assist us in cutting down the time we need. Asking for time is one way to gain a few seconds; seat selection is another way. In my opinion, the best way is to train your mind to have a catalog of plays at the ready.

85

GAMBLING ADDICTION

Do you have any friends, like I do who, after hearing I play some poker, make pointed remarks like, "Do they have a Gambler's Anonymous chapter here in town?" Or, "Can I help you with this addiction?" The point being, they think I have a problem.

These friends are well intentioned. They really have my best interest at heart, but have no real grasp of what a gambling addiction is all about. At one level I am grateful for their concern; at another, it irritates me that they don't have much faith in my ability to know whether or not I have an addiction. Everyone who takes a drink is not an alcoholic. As a point in fact, very few are. It is tragic when it happens, but the percentages are small. Everyone who makes a bet at the track is not an addictive gambler. Very few are. I play poker. I do not regularly play any game that the house has an edge on because I like to win.

A small but significant portion of our population does have a problem with gambling. It is a terrible sickness, a terrible, beastly problem to have. This addiction can take the food from the kids, make the heat bills go unpaid and the cause bill collectors to call you constantly. This addiction can make you lose your home, your friends and your family. It is serious, partner.

The gambling addict's family suffer the most. When the kids go to school with old clothes, they are made fun of by the other kids. When the spouse sits at home worried there will be no money for groceries and rent, there is a problem.

My suggestion, if you *suspect* you might have a problem, is for you to take a good look at yourself. Take inventory. Be excruciatingly honest. Here are some symptoms to look for:

1. You can never leave a winner. (unless the game breaks).
2. You make a secret of your playing.
3. You don't "make plans" to gamble like you make plans to go to the movies.
4. You usually feel remorse over your gambling.
5. You are constantly trying to quit gambling.
6. You take off from important family functions to gamble.
7. You feel driven by a force that is beyond your control.

If two or more of these symptoms apply to you, you might have a problem.

Remember, if you do have a problem, it isn't a situation you can solve by yourself. Believe me, this addiction stuff is serious. You have tried many times to quit and can't. An addiction to gambling can rob you of your money, your respect, your dignity, and your most precious possession — your relationships with your family. *Don't take chances!* Get professional help and make that difficult call to Gamblers Anonymous. Those people have been down the pike and have walked in your sandals for many a mile. They will be gentle, respectful and caring. Most of all, they can help. If you can't find a local chapter, write to Gamblers Anonymous, P.O. Box 17173, Los Angeles, CA 90017.

86

Let Your Good Cards Beat Bad Players

The frustrations of low-limit poker are legion. There are many ways to get beat, and so many events can happen in any low-limit poker game. It is quite common for a fairly decent player to go off the edge because some other player does something dumb and gets lucky. That is just the way life is in low-limit. Terrible beats go with the territory. Your choices are essentially two: go on tilt or learn to accept. I guess there is another option, now that I think about it. You can quit low-limit poker. That last option doesn't appeal to me.

THE BEST CHOICE

The best choice, in my opinion, is to accept the risks of low-limit poker and develop good coping strategies. We have all seen players who get stymied by bad play and try to cope by making either power moves or fancy betting moves. These moves are poor choices in low-limit. If you try to raise people out of the pot they look quite puzzled, look back at their hole cards, check out what cards are showing and then throw in the extra bets. I have found it is close to impossible to move anyone who has any kind of a hand or any kind of a draw. That will include almost everyone at the table. Power moves confuse my fellow players, and they counter that confusion by throwing their money in the pot.

FANCY BETTING

Fancy betting moves seldom work, either. Usually the other player(s) have no idea what correct betting strategy is, and so they are just baffled by anything fancy and will call you down. They will have no idea you made an excellent move and that they should honor that by getting out. They should know that the only person in the world who would make that bet would have the absolute mortal nuts, but they don't know it, so they call you with a pair of fours and win the pot.

TAKE NO PRISONERS

My advice to anyone who plays low-limit poker is to let your cards do the talking. Show nothing but the best hand. Don't try to bluff; don't try to steal the antes or the blinds. Exercise the finest elements of patience. Do not enter pots with anything marginal, throw away busted hands before they start to cost you, and wait until you have your fellow players up against the wall and take their money. When you have them cold, take no prisoners. Extract that last ounce of blood. If they are going all in and want to keep one chip, demand that chip also.

Don't ever taunt them with comments like, "Take that hand over to the shop and get it fixed," "Get a hand," or "How could you play a cheese hand like that against me?" Statements like that are low class and could easily come back to haunt you. Be a class act. Don't whisper to a friend about his or her poor play; just be quiet and stack the chips. Let your cards do the talking. Good cards beat bad players. Nothing more needs to be said.

87

Climb The Mountain Slowly

I recognize that some readers of this book are young pups, while some of us have gray at the temples and gray in the beard, as in my case. While once we thought being 30 was ancient, now 30 is in the distant past. The youngsters get impatient with us guys who take things a little slower, stopping to smell the blossoms and reveling in a sunset.

Let me point out that age has some tremendous advantages that allow us to use a lower gear, charge the mountain a chunk at a time and reflect on past opportunities that looked rosy at the beginning and did not stand the test.

An important lesson for me has been to find a comfortable niche in the learning process. A good bit of my misspent youth was invested in a frontal assault on whatever project appeared to be worthwhile at that moment. Life is an adventure, and I believed I should make the most of each moment and be as efficient as possible. I approached life in the same way I would go about killing a rattlesnake — with great vigor.

I still believe life to be an adventure. However, now my goal is to enjoy the journey and savor the uncertainties and eccentricities.

The big lesson for me has been to enjoy the learning process of whatever enterprise appeals to me. Poker has certainly been an appealing enterprise, and I have enjoyed the process of learning how to become a consistent winner. Fighting my youthful tendencies to charge the hill and learn all I can ASAP, I have chosen the path of leisurely learning. This has worked for me. Maybe it will for you.

I believe you can turn the game of poker into a profitable enterprise if you have certain basic fundamentals firmly within your comprehension. Basic fundamentals include a strict adherence to a list of starting hands, patience to wait for those starting hands, a careful consideration of position, a tight control of marginal hands, a pretty decent betting strategy and emotional control.

Do not think that a grasp of the fundamentals is the same as *mastering* the fundamentals! Especially don't forget the rule that poker is a game of nuances. The subtleties will let your wins go from mediocre to outstanding. So keep that carrot out in front of you. Continue to learn, but now you can do it at a more leisurely pace. Continue to read and think, study and daydream. As you review a hand, ask yourself, "What if I had . . ." Try to find alternate ways of playing. Constantly improve your ability to read other players. Watch for patterns and tells.

THE NICE THINGS IN LIFE

While it is a good idea to keep in mind that poker is a "game", remind yourself of the good things this game can do for you. Things like a better automobile, exquisite furnishings for your home, the latest and best clothes. And don't forget the respect and admiration you will get from your fellow players. Expect these things and they will happen.

88

Don't Get Discouraged

I stood at the entrance of one of the major card rooms in Los Angeles recently and watched the expressions on the faces of people who were leaving. Try it sometime. In thirty minutes you will earn at least three credits from The University of Authentic Poker.

Many of the people headed for the parking lot appeared to be talking to themselves. I wonder why. Were they contemplating what they would have to tell their spouses? Were they cursing under their breath? If so, what were they cursing? Their own bad play? Not likely. Were they cursing a bad beat? Ah, yes. That is quite possible. The bad beat, the guy who didn't have a thing on the flop and stayed to draw for a draw and hit it. The old twenty-four to one shot that beat up on the top set. Or the guy who started with a pair of fours with a three kicker in Seven Card Stud and backed into a flush. Those beats will make a person talk to themselves.

When you listen in on almost any conversation between players, you will hear bad beat stories, stories that will curl your earlobes. Tragic cases will be reported with bleating inflections that beg for sympathy. I say forget it, get a life — a life as a poker winner.

WINNERS DON'T COMPLAIN

I polled several of my friends. We all agree. We don't know a single winning low-limit poker player who complains about bad beats. I invite you to think about that. Why don't consistent winners complain about bad beats? Don't they get any? Sure they do. So why? Winners in low-limit poker have simply trained themselves to ignore the bad beat, the two-card draw to catch perfects when the player had no business in the pot. Winners just shrug their shoulders and get on with the next hand. They clearly avoid thinking about it except to put the other player in the poor player category and deal with him as such.

BRAIN-SAVING TIP

Winning low-limit poker players know that bad beats can penetrate your head and make you lose your concentration. If you lose your focus, you will miss important clues. The brain cells are all needed to analyze what is going on, who is playing loose, who has gone on tilt, etc.

Emotions are crazy things and if you let a bad beat stir your emotions, you will get frustrated and discouraged. Don't let that happen. Use your intellect to override the emotional impact and refuse to even think about that idiot who just got crazy lucky to run down your top set with trash. If you allow yourself to get discouraged, the rest of your game will be impacted. You might get angry and try to get back at that guy who made the stupid play. That will probably cost you some more of your chips. Again, let your intellect take charge and just refuse to get discouraged. Keep alert and play your best game. That will defeat the sloppy play in the long run. You will have ample revenge!

89

A Good Attitude Is The Winner

How important is a good attitude? I say a good attitude is the difference between winning and losing when skill is about equal. Poker skill can, and is, learned. When two people have about the same level of competency, attitude is the deciding factor.

Many poker players are cross. Some are sarcastic and make cutting and hurtful remarks about others and how they play. Some players I have seen are downright nasty to a newcomer, who obviously doesn't yet understand what is going on. If the newcomer is slow to act, the hostile player will actually scream at him or her. For delaying the game because of confusion, the newcomer gets a verbal tongue lashing.

Let me tell you exactly what I believe. These angry, hostile people are losers. Every one of these types, in my opinion, has a real problem with their emotions. An emotional problem almost automatically eliminates a player from becoming a winner. Therefore, I feel I can confidently say "these candy-ass players are losers!"

Consider for a moment that while a person is ridiculing another or that person's play, he is missing a whole bunch of stuff that is going on at the table. His brain is tied up with the frustration he feels and the necessity to put down another. Any poker game I have ever been in demands a strong ability to focus on what others are doing and how you should respond. That ability to focus on the action is a requirement of consistent winning. I must study each player for his habits, trying to detect clues and tells, making estimates on what I think that person is betting or raising on, trying to estimate how well he is able to read the other players, and reviewing how the hand developed when the cards are shown down to get a fix on how each player understands how this game should be played. These are just a very few of the things that each player should notice as the game progresses.

THINK POSITIVE

We all need to add information into our mental "book" as to which player is a calling station, which ones will call down a hand with a small pair, who will raise with a draw, who will bet into a dangerous board, who plays only quality cards, who will try to bluff, etc. If you have your brain cells all tied up thinking up smart things to put down others, you will miss a lot of stuff you should be picking up. The analysis of each hand could be very important later when you are contesting for the pot.

Besides missing clues and information, derogatory players have to deal with stomach acid. A positive attitude projected to others is so much easier on our bodies and spirits. A warm and accepting demeanor makes you into a person who is pleasant to be around and who is appreciated at the table. Being grouchy certainly doesn't help you find friends.

90

Be Open To Friendships

One of the truly rewarding aspects of living is the development of friendships. Rewarding, not in the financial sense at all, but in the most real area of emotional maturation. Friends bring real joy to us. Friends are there for us when the going gets tough. Friends have our best interests at heart and try to give us accurate information about ourselves. In this uncertain vale of tears, friends provide great stability. When we need a hand up, a friend is there.

My goal in this chapter is not to glorify or romanticize friendship. (And I draw a line between friendship and acquaintanceship. Friendships require time and energy, not the mere passing of time.) The idea I want to get across is the value of friendships that can be developed at the poker table(s).

Let me tell you about Steve. Steve has long hair and is a thespian. Steve is a quiet type of person who is in heavy concentration while at the poker table. I mean this guy doesn't eat, drink or talk while engaged in poker. Once in a while he will grunt. Usually the grunt is just before he mucks his cards after another player has shown him a better hand.

Steve and I have been friends for years. We often do not see each other for months. We talk on the phone occasionally. What we have going for the friendship is trust. I trust Steve to help me think through a problem, either personal or with a card puzzle. He is smart and sensitive, and he will put his very best effort into helping me.

Steve is a good illustration of the type of friendship that can happen over the green felt.

WARM FUZZIES

When we work on presenting a warm, friendly image at the table, we open up possibilities for friendships. I can just hear someone out there grousing that they play poker to win money, not run a popularity program. You can do both. In fact, being friendly and offering a smile will definitely help your game. A smile is the vehicle to fostering friendship. Being friendly will make you a more positive person, which will enhance your ability to think clearly.

Keep your focus on winning but also be open to finding a person who can add the riches of friendship to your life.

You can be a:

AND a:

91

The Heart Of The Matter

Sometimes, after I have a good hand beaten, I wish that poker was like video poker. When you make a good hand, you get paid! On other occasions, after I have pulled off a steal, I am extremely grateful that poker is not like video poker. My nothing hand would have won nothing on a machine, but through skill and a bit of luck, I was stacking chips.

I often contend that poker is not a card game, but a people game played with cards and chips. And the heart of the game, the bottom line, is our skill or ability to know when we have the better hand. (I agree that on a very few occasions, the heart of the matter is the ability to make our opponent think we have the better hand.)

COMPARISON IS THE KEY

Knowing when to call, when to raise and when to fold are totally based upon the comparison of what we have versus what we think the other player or players have. That is the heart of the matter, the skill of the game. That comparison is what makes us winners at the end of the year.

Suppose I have the ace and king of hearts in a Texas Hold 'Em game. The flop comes with an ace, a seven and a three. Three different suits, no hearts. I bet and am called in two places. "What can they have to call my bet?" I ask myself. Maybe an ace with a bad kicker, maybe a draw for a draw, as is quite common in low-limit poker. The jack of hearts comes on the turn. I bet and get raised! Then the other player calls the raise cold! Now what do I do? What kind of hands can I put them on? More to the point, what hands can I put them on that I can beat? The comparison of my hand to theirs is the heart of the matter. My evaluation of the players and the texture of the flop is where skill comes into play. Should I throw my top pair away? Should I re-raise? Should I call? I know very little about either man's play. I make the assumption that since the other player called the raise cold, one of them has at least two pairs, probably trips with that kind of flop texture. I muck my hand and save some dollars. At the showdown, the raiser had three threes and the other player had an ace-jack. I was beat in two places.

BASIC TOOLS

My point in this hypothetical situation is not that I am a clever player. My aim is to guide you to always make the comparison between your hand and those of the other players! You might have a poor hand, but it might be the best hand in that particular deal. Recognizing when you can win the hand and when you are beaten is the skill to work on after you have become knowledgeable about starting hand selection, position and patience. Hand selection, position and patience are the basic tools of your game of poker. When you become proficient with these tools, you will be a winner.

92

Do You Have A Tell?

Do you have a tell or tells? Every good poker player has asked that question of themselves. It is pretty scary to think that you are giving away the contents of your hand(s). Can you imagine how much money it has cost you if you do have a consistent tell?

I'm fairly sure that most of us have one or more gestures or habits that give away some information to the astute observer. I have discovered a couple of tells that I had and have worked to remove. It is an advantage for low-limit poker players that most low-limit opponents are not terribly observant. Most of the competitors we will encounter have not developed their own style of play to the point where they can detect subtle clues about your play. However, that should not stop us from doing our best to discover and eliminate any tell we might have. If we lose even one big pot a month because of a tell, it will cost us quite a bit of money.

One of my tells happened when I had raised before the flop in Texas Hold 'Em with, say, the ace-king. If there was no help on the flop, I would quickly make a bet to try to intimidate the players into folding. The quick action was the tell. When I had a good hand, my actions were a fraction slower. When this was pointed out to me, I was able to modify that quick action. Now I make a conscious effort to have a consistent pattern to my betting. Some days I will bet quickly regardless of the strength of my hand, while betting extremely slow on other days, regardless of the strength of my hand. Sometimes I will carefully stack my bet in front of me; other times I will toss the chips. Sometimes I will say, "I will just bet this one time." This is obviously a ploy to get callers, and I will say it whether I plan to bet only once or all the way to the river. After the players have seen and heard that I will say, "I will just bet this one time" when I have a weak hand and I don't want callers. While the words are exactly the same, my tactic at this point is to get people to fold marginal hands.

HOW DO YOU DETECT A TELL IN YOURSELF?

I think the best insurance against a tell is to have a trusted friend watch you play, and you watch him and compare notes. This is how I discovered that "quick action" tell. This seems to me to be the most efficient way because a tell is difficult for you to recognize in yourself. When you do this, it also helps you focus on all your actions and you become more aware of how you are coming across to others.

Another way to try to detect a tell in yourself is to reflect on your actions after a big pot has been played out. Review each motion carefully and the force of each motion. As Mike Caro, The Mad Genius of Poker, writes in his *Book Of Tells*, strong means weak and weak means strong. So if a person throws his chips out in an intimidating and forceful way, it could be that he is bluffing or doesn't want any callers. If he just carefully, almost apologetically, lays the chips on the felt, he usually will have a very good hand and he wants you to call or raise. Look for those kinds of actions in yourself. If you try to bully people off the pot with actions or words when you have a weak hand, you have a tell. The thing to do when you discover a tell is to do just the opposite for a while until the observant players realize your tell is being used against them.

93

Recognize When You Are Beaten

A costly mistake many, many players make is the failure to unload a hand when you are defeated. I think part of that refusal to surrender a good hand is ego, part of it is hope that you will get lucky, and part of it is plain ordinary garden-variety stubbornness.

THE BIG PAIRS

I have seen some incredible examples of playing dead hands. The other night a guy played a pair of red jacks to the bitter, and I mean bitter, end. The game was Texas Hold 'Em, and the flop had the ace of spades, the king of spades and the seven of hearts. He bet first and was raised. He called the raise. The seven of spades came on the turn and he called three bets to see the last card. That card was the three of spades. Again, he called three bets. You have to ask, "What could he possibly beat?" The guy with sevens full of aces took the pot, and the guy with the nut flush showed his hand before he mucked it.

You see lots of strange things in low-limit poker. In a Seven Card Stud game, Pete had two pairs, kings and sixes. There were two good, tough players in the game and both had four cards to a suit, each with a king on the board; one of them had a six showing. Ralph was boxed between their raises but called them all. He was drawing a one card, his only out to make a full house.

These are examples of obscene calls. It is seldom that easy to know that you are beaten as in these two illustrations. Most of the time the clues are much more subtle. Because of the wacky nature of low-limit poker, it is more difficult to recognize dangerous situations. I am fully sympathetic to the problems of accurately putting a bad player on a hand. However, reading the players and the unique circumstance of each hand is a skill that will make us a lot of money, or in the case of the above two examples, save us a lot.

POKER PLAYERS AND THEIR EGOS

Let's be clear that there is more to recognizing when to get out than reading the players. As mentioned, ego is certainly a factor. Poker players, by and large, have big egos. They consider themselves decent to good players. When we allow our egos to affect our judgments at the table, quite often we take a hit in the wallet. That is a fact.

Garden-variety stubbornness will also usually cost you dollars. Stubbornness is not good. To my knowledge no one has figured out a foolproof way to avoid situations in which another player catches his magic card and creams your flush. So if you stay with a hand that is obviously beaten after a dangerous card hits the board and the betting demonstrates clearly that it was the magic card, you are allowing stubbornness to affect your judgment.

Obviously there are other factors that should be recognized for playing a hand after it is apparent that you are beaten: becoming enamored with big pairs, ego, and stubbornness are the most flagrant. When we recognize those components within ourselves, we must empower our rational side to modify the effects and refuse to lose money to those demons.

94

Who Is Your Toughest Opponent?

Stop for a moment and visualize the faces of your toughest opponents. What makes them tough? Do they check-raise? Do they put fear in your heart when they bet? Do they have the reputation of being the very best players around? What makes them good players?

May I suggest to you that your toughest opponent is not Bob, The Brick, or Polish Steve. I suggest that your biggest opponent is you, the guy who looks at you in the mirror every single day. The person who deprives you of the most money at the poker table is *you*.

Now that I have your dander up, your nose open, let me defend my statement. Almost all of us play too many hands. Do you? I would suspect that you would say that you have a good hand-selection process. We all get caught up in the action of the game. We all tend to play marginal hands in marginal situations. We look down at those starting cards and we try to think of reasons to play. What we should do is think of reasons *not* to play the hand. But do we? Hell, no. We love the action. We love the competition. We love to hammer that so and so over there. We love to take chances. We came to *gamble!*

Let's face it, we have difficulty believing we are not good poker players. Our ego tells us we are good. Since we are good poker players, the decisions we make must, by definition, be good decisions. Elementary, right? Wrong.

I truly believe that poker is such a complicated game involving both cards, chips and people that very few are truly accomplished players. Almost all of us have a long way to go. There is so much to this game and it takes a long time and a lot of dedication to become a top player.

POKER IS VERY COMPLEX

Just a few days ago, I was in California playing at a satellite tournament. I saw some absolutely fantastic moves by a couple of players. Because the situation is so dynamic, where every single hand is different from the last, where so many different personality interacting, the possibilities of the same situation happening twice in one lifetime is almost impossible. Every hand the chip count in each hand is different. Each player has a different mind set than the hand before. My point is that there is so much to learn that we must continue to focus on the game in order to become a top player. If we do not consistently focus, we become our toughest opponent.

Some players are their own toughest opponent because they cannot forgive themselves for a bad play. Some players force themselves to play with anger or hatred toward another player. It isn't the other person who is the tough opponent, it is the person who cannot get over a slight or a bad beat.

Some players play too long and lose their sharpness. Some players insist on playing the big pairs far too long when the board tells them they are beat. Not listening or seeing what is happening turns you into a bad adversary.

These are but a few of the many, many ways we do damage to ourselves. Constant dedication to learning and improvement are the only ways I know to decrease the impact of our own egos.

95

Master The Cards Or The Cards Will Master You

Control is something we all want. Control of our destiny, control of our income, control of the automobile, even control of our relationships. When we have control, we feel safe. Feeling safe is good. We like that feeling.

In a poker game, controling or mastering the cards is difficult, but achievable. In fact, if we do not control or master the cards we play, we will lose.

What does it mean to master the cards? It doesn't mean to control the cards that are dealt to you. No one can do that. Controlling the cards means to control which cards we play from which positions. For instance, I was dealt a pair of split nines in a Seven Card Stud game. The lady to my right had the low card showing and was forced to bring it in for one dollar. I checked the board, and there were no nines showing. However, this table had some loose players who liked to raise on almost any kind of draw. There was an ace, a king and two queens showing and yet to act. I threw my hand away. Normally I will play those nines, but I don't want to call a raise with them. My position was most precarious, and it was my choice to abandon the hand and not risk a raise or even two raises to see the next card. If I had been in late position, say the forced opener was to my left and there were no raises, I would certainly have called, maybe even raised if I sensed weakness around the table. This scenario is an example of control.

Some players will automatically call with any pair, large or small. If they have that automatic reaction, they are allowing the cards to control them, not the other way around. They are reacting to the cards. The decisions we make to play or not to play, to raise or to fold, should be based on our experience and judgment. If we have some automatic calls, we are not in control.

MAKE THE CARDS YOUR SERVANTS

Another example of automatic betting is the inability to lay down a hand that is beaten. Playing a pair of queens against a pair of aces or kings is an example of being out of control. I remember a dear lady named Margaret who took a poker class from me. We were playing Seven Card Stud in class and she caught an open pair of queens. Another player had an open pair of kings. She called his bet. I asked her why. She replied, "Maybe I will catch another queen." I carefully explained to her that the other player had the exact same chance to catch another king as she had to catch a queen. I told her, "When you are beaten, get out!" To retire from the action is the move to control the cards and your game. Sure, those queens look great, but when they are beaten, they look like costly possessions. Very costly possessions. Play the cards, control the cards, master the cards and they will be very kind to you.

96

Trouble Hands Spell
T-R-O-U-B-L-E

Can you make a list of trouble hands? Say in the game of Texas Hold 'Em, would your list include ace-queen offsuit? It should. If the game is Seven Card Stud, would you list three-five-eight of clubs? You should. These are dangerous cards. How about in Seven Card Stud, High/Low Split, when you have two of clubs, the five of hearts and your door card is eight of spades? Is that a trouble hand?

These are just a very, very few examples of the hands that spell t-r-o-u-b-l-e. Trouble hands can cost you a lot of money when you have some improvement on the next card. They can trap you if there is a raise after you put your money in the pot. Whatever game you play, I suggest that you make your own list of trouble hands, hands that can bleed your bankroll.

Please note that I am not saying that you should never play trouble hands. By no means! Trouble hands can be played under certain circumstances. Here are my rules for difficult hands:

Rule One: *Only play a trouble hand when you have a good, real good, position.* For example, when I am last to act or when the person to my left are either passive players or have indicated they are about to fold their hands. As you have seen, a lot of players will pick up their cards and let you know they intend to muck the

201

cards. This tell helps you make a decision regarding hands that are on your trouble list.

BE CAREFUL, NOT SHY

Trouble hands *can* show a profit, depending on the circumstances. Don't automatically throw them away. Be on the alert for situations in which you can either play or raise to put pressure on the players who have ragged in. I know this is a bit dangerous in low-limit poker, but if you have a solid reputation as a player, you can get by with a bit of chicanery. After all, you are not exactly barefoot. Suppose you have a queen-four suited on the button in Texas Hold 'Em. Two players call the blind bet. You certainly have a marginal hand but a raise might drive out one of the blinds and give you control of the hand. The players will usually check to the raiser so you will probably get to look at the flop and the turn with no more cost. You might even get lucky and catch a flop with a pair of fours. No one would put you on four so you would get some action and would sow some seeds of confusion in the minds of your fellow players.

Rule Two: *Playing a trouble hand, do not get into a position where you'll lose a lot of money.* If the next card or the flop is not favorable, I will knuckle or muck. Unless there is improvement, no further contribution will be made to protect the first investment. If I should get some improvement, I will certainly make a value judgment at that point based upon my estimate of who is playing what.

Trouble hands can be t-r-o-u-b-l-e or they can be modestly profitable. Take care.

97

Low-Limit Poker Can Be
Hazardous To Your Health

Low-limit poker has not made the surgeon general's list of hazardous pastimes, yet. However, low-limit poker can do you serious mental harm, perhaps irreparable damage. When you flop the Broadway straight and some buffoon over there draws two perfect cards to catch a spade flush with only one spade of the flop (he has an eight-five of spades in his hand!!!), you might say some rather nasty things. At least, you will think some nasty thoughts, question his ancestry or place a curse on his children.

These kinds of beats are pretty average beats in low-limit poker. These defeats go with the territory, occupational hazards with which we must cope or they will rob us of our fair share of the chips. If we let these beats send us off the end of the pier, we are acknowledging we cannot beat this game. When we gripe, grouse, mumble and groan, we are saying that these events are beyond our ability to endure. I say to you, do not, repeat, do not, let horrible hits put you out of control. Then the turkeys are in charge of the house. Be prepared! Do your mental homework so that when that inevitable beat catches you, it does not find you poorly equipped to handle it.

Then the questions become, "What is mental homework?" and "How do you do that mental homework?"

Mental homework is made up of several things. I believe the most important aspect is to know that beats will happen so that you therefore do not become angry when they occur. When I was a kid on the farm, I had to collect the eggs. When a hen was sitting on the nest and I tried to slip my hand under her to get the eggs, she would peck at my hand. I became angry at her until I realized that that is what chickens are supposed to do. Their instinct is to protect the nest. From then on I either wore a glove or turned my palm upward so that the peck would not hurt so much. I learned how to cope.

Another example of mental homework is a watchdog. Watch dogs protect property. When you must go on to property protected by a watch dog, you will be smart to call ahead and ask the owner to restrain the dog. Otherwise you could pay the price in the seat of your britches.

Another protective element is knowing that these guys who put on bad beats are losers. They are drawing against horrendous odds. When you play good cards from good position, you will win in the long run. In fact, these guys are a main source of income for you. They contribute generously to the game. Welcome them, encourage them. They have no idea that the lucky hit they get occasionally will cost them dearly in the long run.

My personal experience with bad beats has shown me that I can deal with three of them in any one session. If I should get a fourth one, I can feel my equilibrium start to slip. I keep track of those beats now and if that fourth one hits, I will get up and leave. I have maxed out my tolerance for that day. If I stay in the game, I could lose control, which could cost me some chips.

98

Ego, Ego, Ego

As I watch the action around a poker table in the card rooms in California, in the casinos in Nevada, and the play here in Colorado, I am amazed at the level of ego displayed. This ego is usually confined to males. It seems to me that the "other sex," fair and beautiful as they are, has more sense than to place their bankroll in jeopardy by taking a firm stand in the face of adversity and almost certain defeat. That good old male ego can cost a player a bunch of money over the course of a year or so. The message in this chapter is to take a close look at our own egos and try to evaluate what effect that ego has on our play at the table.

Ego gets involved with our play when we take a modest hand or even a poor one and try to power it through some tough opponents. Let me illustrate what I mean. Say this guy calls before the flop with the ace-three of spades. The flop comes with an ace in it, say, ace-nine-four of different suits. The guy bets and gets raised and another guy calls. Now what would you do? What could they have that you could beat? You found out what you wanted to know. Get out. Oh, no. Not this guy. He has an ace and he will show the hand down. That is ego. Dumb.

Lots of poker players think they have the courage of a pirate. They don't flinch when looking into the business end of a cannon or blink when a bully snarls. But give them a poor hand and all the evidence in the world that they are beat, and they will still call the hand down. They must think that is bravery.

The other night Carole was sitting next to me and she check-raised a guy. The game was Texas Hold 'Em. The flop came ten-ten-six. Carole was in third position. She checked, everyone checked except the dealer. He threw in a bet in a defiant manner. She check-raised. Everyone folded except our hero. He groused but threw in his money. The next card was nothing. Carole bet again. The champion again called with an angry gesture. The last card was an ace and I figured it gave Carole a full house. She bet and, of course, the guy called. She showed him her boat and asked to see his hand. He had the king-seven of hearts and there was only one heart on the board. Guess what? His ego made him do it. He just refused to believe she had him beat. I guess he could not believe that a woman could beat him.

THE MESSAGE WAS NOT IN CODE!

Carole told him exactly what she had with her check-raise. What more information could the guy expect? Carole was a solid player who played solid cards. Knowing that it usually is a bad practice in low-limit poker, she seldom bluffed. Yet all that guy could beat would be a stone bluff.

This game of poker seems to bring out the ego in all of us. If you see yourself in these stories, have a little talk with yourself. You are costing yourself some money.

99

Do You Play Or Do You Play To Win?

Roger was a fun player to have in the game. He was a big jolly guy who just loved to play poker. We called him Roger Funbucks. The game always picked up when he sat down. He would stay with the most incredible cards from any position. Trying to put him on a hand was like throwing rocks at the moon. Roger Funbucks played each hand to the end, saying, "You have to give those cards a chance." Roger played to play. He made a good deal of money on his job and he worked hard. So when he came to play, he played. He would throw off three to four hundred and get up and leave. As I said, we loved it when he came to play.

If you feel that way about poker, terrific. I don't understand why you are reading this book though. This book is about winning, remember? One hundred one ways to *win*.

I have absolutely no objection to anyone who wants to make poker a fun experience. However, I have more fun when I win. So winning is my goal, so that I can have fun. And then I also have fun with the money I win. A double bonus. Fun to win and fun with the money. What a deal, right?

The lifeblood of any game are the players who are not too worried about doing the homework required to win. Those are the guys I am nice to. They support my habit of buying good clothes. Sure, I know it takes energy and focus to learn this game so that either the money lasts longer or, so help me Myrtle, I become a winner in the long term.

An example of a player who has gone from being a recreation player who threw off his money to one who consistently wins was Frank. We all loved Frank in the old days. He took his teamster wages and deposited them at the green felt. He played seven of ten hands, he played all night, he drew to long shots and once in a while he actually left winners. I don't know when he woke up and smelled the caffeine, but one day I noticed he only played once or twice a round. When he played to end, he showed down a quality hand that usually won the pot. "What the hell happened to Frank?" we started to ask. What used to be a donator had become a shark. He was taking money instead of contributing. Who the hell did he think he was anyway?

Frank told me that he just got fed up with playing for recreation and giving away his money. He wanted to have more bang for his buck, and he ended up being a winning player. From sucker to success.

I think it boils down to the choice we make as to what we want out of the game. Are we willing to pay the price of conquest, or do we just want to have some fun, spend a little and go home? After all, it costs money to take your wife out to dinner, to see the opera, to watch the Rams play. Why not have some fun at a little game of chance? Everything costs money, so why should anyone object to the price of admission? And once in a while you will hit a lick and leave winners. God bless, I say. Either way is fine. Just make your choice. Play to play or play to win. Your choice. America is a great country.

100

Trapped By Second Best

What is the most expensive hand in poker? Every poker player worth his salt knows it is the second best hand. They don't pay off for second at the track. It is not only the financial cost, but also the embarrassment. I still shudder to think of the times when the showdown was three handed and I was the bottom dog in that pile. Oh, it hurt. At that moment, if I had not been too lazy to work and too chicken to steal, I would have given up poker forever.

In low-limit poker, there is so much chasing. Chasing is when you should know that you have a second or third best, but stay to try to catch a card that will make you the winner. Say you have a buried pair of sevens in Seven Card Stud. You call and a good player pairs his door card, a ten, on the next card. He bets and you call. Why on earth would you call? Yet it happens all the time. He certainly has the better hand, and even if you should catch a seven, God forbid, you are probably still way behind.

Suppose you have that rag hand of a pair of jacks in Texas Hold 'Em. The flop comes king-six-six. It is bet and raised before it gets back to you. What out there can you beat? Yet most low-limit players will call with those shabby jacks. (Of course, you should call if the pot is big enough, which it seldom is.)

Let me quote a dear old friend who is a guru to me at the poker table. He has said, "Why draw to a hand that you cannot raise with if you hit it?" Think about that and apply it to your play. Most of us are so anxious to play that we take almost any old draw hand and try to get lucky (like for example, the player who will play a nine-three of hearts, hoping for a heart flush in Texas Hold 'Em). Even if you should catch your flush (about a 5 percent shot), you would be afraid to raise with it. So why play it?

THERE IS NO SILVER MEDAL IN POKER

The same concept of avoiding second best hands in Seven Card Stud is to not draw at a straight when another player has three to a suit showing on fifth street. Why do it? If he bets or raises, get out. Even if you make the straight, you can't raise with it. Second best is trouble. Expensive trouble. Avoid those circumstances if at all possible.

It is terribly important to recognize where you are at in each and every hand of poker. You can usually avoid trouble if you select quality starting hands and improve quickly. If you don't improve, strongly consider retiring. If you should play modest or marginal hands and don't make a drastic improvement, get out. Low-limit poker has enough dangers without tempting fate. Don't be the one caught going uphill. Make the turkeys try to catch you, not the other way around. Stay away from second best!

101

Early Position Is For Losers

Few, good poker players, if any make money from early position. That is a fact. Sure, there is the exception when you hit a big pair, raise and get it heads-up against one other player. However, you will make only a few bucks even if you should win. Those situations are rare in the long term.

In fixed position games, like Texas Hold 'Em and Omaha, you have an opportunity to avoid either the temptation to play or, in games with an ante, like in California, you can get up and walk around when you are in front of the blinds. You will save a few dollars over the course of a few hours' play. In games that have random position play, such as Seven Card Stud, you do not have that opportunity. If the guy on your right is forced to bring it in, you are in a bad position for at least that betting round. There is no way to know in advance about your position.

The main reason early position is for losers is that you can't or shouldn't get paid for holding a marginal hand. As you know, there are a whole lot more marginal hands than premium hands. A whole lot more. A pair of nines in Seven Card Stud is a marginal hand. If you catch that pair of nines in early position, you should muck it if there is any danger it will be raised. If you catch that same pair of nines in late or last position, it is playable, maybe even okay for a raising hand, depending on the circumstances. There is no change in the hand itself, but the position makes it demonstratively more valuable. The value added is position. If the pot is raised before the action gets to you, throw it away. If a couple of players just call with low cards showing, a raise is justified.

In Texas Hold 'Em, you should never play a king-jack offsuit in early position. That same king-jack is a raising hand on or just in front of the button if there has been no previous raise. Again, no change in the rank of the cards, just a value added because of position. If you catch a flop where no one makes a hand, a bet will usually buy the pot for you.

TEST OUT THIS IDEA

If you play in a Texas Hold 'Em game with an ante, such as they have in California, you have an option that I suggest. Say the $3-$6 game is nine handed. The blinds will cost you one dollar and three dollars. That figures out to about 44 cents per hand, right? In addition, there is a fifty-cent ante that disappears down the hatch. Since you can only play a very few hands in the two positions before the blinds get to you, why not take a walk and avoid the fifty-cent-a-hand ante for those two hands? Make your trip to the bathroom, talk briefly with a friend, visit with the floorman, order a cup of coffee. Just get a brief bit of exercise. Get back just in time for your blinds and save a few bucks. Those hands are not worth fifty cents and you will not be tempted to play marginal hands like ten-jack suited, hands that you don't want to see raised behind you. The same technique works in Omaha.

GLOSSARY

Here are some poker expressions that are fairly common. Naturally, like all of language, the definitions change and mean different things in different localities. This is a guide.

ACES UP

Two pair, one of which is a pair of Aces.

ACTIVE PLAYER

A player still involved in the pot.

ALL BLUE OR ALL PINK

A flush

BABY

A small card, usually five or less.

BACK DOOR

When a player makes a hand he wasn't drawing at.

BACK-RAISE

A re-raise.

BAD BEAT

When a big hand is beaten by someone who drew to a longshot.

BELLY-BUSTER STRAIGHT

Also called an inside straight draw.

BICYCLE

The lowest possible hand in Lowball.

BIG BLIND

The second (sometimes the third) Blind bet.

BIG DOG

A hand that is the underdog to win the hand.

BIG FULL

The best possible full house.

BLANK

A card that is not of value to a player's hand.

BLUFF

An attempt to win the pot by betting without having a winning hand.

BOARD

Any cards that are placed face up during a game.

BOXED CARD

A card in the deck that faces the wrong way.

BROADWAY

An Ace high straight.

BULL THE GAME

When a very aggressive player bets, raises and re-raises.

BULLET

An Ace

BURN AND TURN

To discard the top card and deal the next card(s) to the players or to place them in the center of the table.

BURN CARD

The top card that is discarded.

BUSTED HAND

A worthless hand.

BUTTON

An object to indicate who is the dealer. It passes clockwise around the table.

BUY-IN

The minimum required to enter a game.

CALLING STATION

A player who will call almost any bet but will seldom bet.

CARDS SPEAK

A form of High-Low poker where the cards are placed face up at the conclusion of the hand. Instead of the player "declaring" one way or both ways, the cards speak.

CASE CARD

The last card of a particular rank left in the deck.

CATCH PERFECT

In a long shot draw, the player catches the card he needs.

CHANGE GEARS

Changing your style of play.

CHASE

Trying to beat a hand that is better than yours.

CHECK BLIND

To check without looking at the hand.

CHECK-RAISE

To check and then raise when the action gets back around. Sometimes there are rules against this.

COMMON CARD

A card or cards placed face up in the center that can be used by all the players.

COMPLETE BLUFF

A bluff made with a worthless hand.

CONCEALED PAIR

A pair where both cards are face down.

COWBOY

A King

CRIPPLE THE DECK

When you have such a good hand that no one can beat you.

CRYING CALL

To make a very marginal call.

DARK BET

To bet without looking at your hand.

DEAD HAND

A hand that has been fouled or has too many or too few cards.

DEALER'S CHOICE

A poker game where the dealer chooses what game to play.

DECLARE

A form of High-Low where the person must declare which way his hand will play. See Cards Speak.

DOG

The underdog. Opposite of the favorite.

DOOR-CARD

The first up card in Stud poker.

DOUBLE BELLY BUSTER

A situation where one of two cards will make an inside straight. In Hold 'Em, you have Jack-five and the flop comes 7-8-9. Any six or ten will give you a straight.

DOUBLE-POP

When the second player re-raises a raise.

DOWN TO THE GREEN

When a player has gone all in.

DRAWING DEAD

Drawing at a hand that even if you make it, you cannot possibly win.

DRAW-OUT

To improve your hand and beat an opponent who originally had a better hand.

EARLY, MIDDLE AND LATE POSITION

Refers to the different positions during a hand. Early are the first three players to act, middle the next three or four, and late are those closest to the button.

EDGE

An advantage

EXPOSED PAIR

An exposed pair, as opposed to a split pair or a hidden pair.

FAMILY POT

A pot where everyone at the table is involved.

FAST

Playing a hand as aggressively as possible.

FIFTH STREET

In Hold 'Em, it is the last card exposed. In Stud, it is the fifth card dealt.

FISH

An easy player.

FLOORMAN

The supervisor in a card room.

FLOP

In Hold 'Em, the flop is the three community cards placed face up by the dealer.

FLOPPING A SET

In Hold 'Em, when you have a pair in the hole and one of your cards comes on the flop.

FLUSH

Five cards of one suit.

FOUR-FLUSH

Four cards in one suit.

FOURTH STREET
In Hold 'Em games, it is the fourth community card exposed by the dealer. In Stud, it is the fourth card dealt.

FREE-CARD
Everyone gets a card when no one bets during a betting round.

FULL HOUSE
Three of a kind and a pair.

GETTING A HAND CRACKED
When a big hand is beaten by someone who drew out on it.

GUT SHOT
An inside straight draw.

GRIFTER
A cheat

HEAD-UP
Two players competing.

HIGH ROLLER
A player who plays big stakes.

HOOK
A Jack

IGNORANT END OF A STRAIGHT
The lower end of a straight in a game that has community cards.

IN THE LEAD
The player who is the first to bet.

IN THE MIDDLE
A player caught between the better and a potential raiser. A tough place to be.

IN THE POCKET
Hole cards

JAM
A pot where several players are raising.

KIBITZER

A spectator.

KICKER

In Hold 'Em, when one of your hole cards is paired on the board, your other card is a kicker.

KICKER TROUBLE

When you have a weak kicker to go with a pair.

LEATHER ASS

Refers to a player who is patient.

LIMP IN

To call a bet.

LITTLE BLIND

The first and smallest of the blinds.

LIVE STRADDLE

When the player in front of the blinds puts up an optional blind. He also has the option of raising when the action gets back to him.

LOCAL

A Las Vegas resident.

LOCK

A hand that cannot lose. Also called the "Mortal Nuts."

LOOKING DOWN HIS THROAT

Knowing that you can't be beat.

LOOSE PLAYER

A player who gets involved with a lot of hands.

MECHANIC

A cheat who can manipulate the cards to deal himself or another a good hand.

MISS THE FLOP

When your two cards in Hold 'Em do not correlate with the flop.

MUCK

The discards

NUT PLAYER

A very tight player who plays only the best hands.

NUTS

The best hand possible at that point.

OFF-SUIT

In Hold 'Em, refers to the two hole cards that are not of the same suit.

OMAHA

A form of Hold 'Em where each player is dealt four cards. The player has to use two of those cards in his final five cards.

ON THE COME

Not a complete hand. Many players bet "on the come."

ON TILT

A term referring to a player who is playing badly.

OPEN-END STRAIGHT

Four consecutive cards.

OUTS

A term that refers to the number of cards that can help your hand.

OVERCALL

To call a bet after another player has called.

OVERPAIR

In Hold 'Em, a pair in the pocket that is higher than any card on the board.

PAINT

A face card.

PICKED OFF

To get called when you are bluffing.

PIECE OF CHEESE

Can refer to an easy play or it can refer to a bad hand.

PIGEON
An easy player.

PLAY-BACK
Re-raise

PLAY BEHIND
When a player, before he looks at his hand, declares that he will bring more money into the game.

PLAYING OVER
When a player temporarily leaves his seat and another player will sit in until the first player returns.

POT ODDS
The relation of the amount of money in the pot compared to the amount of money necessary to call.

PREMIUM HANDS
The best possible hands.

PUPPY FEET
Clubs

PUT A PLAY ON
To attempt to win by out-maneuvering an opponent.

RAGS
Poor cards

RAKE
The percentage of the pot taken by the casino or house.

RAT-HOLE
To take money or chips off the table during play.

READ
The attempt to guess what an opponent has.

REPRESENT
 To attempt to make an opponent believe you have a hand that you don't have.

RIBBON CLERK
 A small time gambler.

RING GAME
 A full game.

RIVER CARD
 The last card dealt.

ROCK
 A good player, usually conservative.

ROLLED UP
 In Seven-Card Stud, the description of first three cards that make trips.

RUSH
 A winning streak.

SANDBAG
 Slow playing a good hand with the intention of raising later.

SCOOP
 To win both ends in a High-Low game.

SECOND BUTTON
 The second pair.

SECOND NUT
 The second best possible hand.

SEMI-BLUFF
 Basically a bluffing play, which has some outs that could win.

SET
 Three of a kind, trips.

SHILL
 A house player who plays with house money.

SHORT-HANDED GAME
 A game not full.

SIXTH STREET
   The sixth card dealt in Stud.

SLOW-PLAY
   To let other players take the lead in betting.

SNAPPED OFF
   To get a good hand beat.

SOLID PLAYER
   A strong, all around player.

SPEEDING AROUND
   Applies to a loose player who doesn't know what he is doing.

SPLIT PAIR
   A pair in Stud with one card up and the other down.

STAY
   To call or raise.

STEAL POSITION
   The next to last or last position.

STRING BET
   An illegal way of betting. A bet has to be made in one motion. A string bet is when a player makes a partial bet and watches for a reaction from the other players. If he gets the reaction he wants, he will complete the bet or raise.

SUCKER
   A player who likes to play a lot of hands. He plays hands that should not be played.

TAP
   Going all-in table stakes poker.

TELL
   A clue that reveals what a player has in his hand.

THIRD STREET
   In Stud, the third card dealt.

TIED ON

When your hand is good enough to play it to the end.

TIGHT PLAYER

A person who plays only the premium hands.

TOKE

A tip.

TOP PAIR

In Hold 'Em, when the highest card on the board matches one of your hole cards.

TURKEY

A sucker.

UNDERFULL

A full house that is not the biggest possible full house.

UNDER THE GUN

The first player to act.

UPHILL

To chase or try to outdraw a better hand.

WELCHER

A player who fails to pay a debt.

WHEEL

See Bicycle.

WIRED PAIR

The first two cards are a pair.

Order Form

You can order this book or any of Andy Nelson's books on poker simply by filling out this order blank. Be assured that all books are 100 percent guaranteed. If you don't like them for any reason, return them within thirty days and receive your money back, no questions asked.

☐ Yes, please send me POKER - 101 WAYS TO WIN
☐ Please send me these books by Andy Nelson: (See second page in front of book for list)

_____

_____

_____

_____

☐ Please send me a current list of Andy Nelson's books on poker.

(We will also enclose a few of Andy's latest TIPS AND TRICKS)

Name _____

Address _____

City, State, Zip_____

Make check out to: POKERBOOK PRESS
P.O. Box 17851, Boulder, Colorado 80308
Please add $2.00 shipping and handling for the first book and 75 cents for each additional book. We try to ship on a next day basis, but sometimes it takes three to four weeks for delivery through the mails. Thanks!